ABORTIO

The fight for reproductive rights

Judith Orr

First published in Great Britain in 2017 by

Policy Press
University of Bristol
1-9 Old Park Hill
Bristol
BS2 8BB
UK
t: +44 (0)117 954 5940
pp-info@bristol.ac.uk
www.policypress.co.uk

North America office:
Policy Press
c/o The University of Chicago Press
1427 East 60th Street
Chicago, IL 60637, USA
t: +1 773 702 7700
f: +1 773 702 9756
sales@press.uchicago.edu
www.press.uchicago.edu

British Library Cataloguing in Publication Data
A catalogue record for this book is available from the British Library.

Library of Congress Cataloging-in-Publication Data
A catalog record for this book has been requested.

ISBN 978-1-4473-3911-3 paperback
ISBN 978-1-4473-3913-7 ePub
ISBN 978-1-4473-3914-4 Mobi
ISBN 978-1-4473-3912-0 ePdf

Cover design by Lyn Davies
Front cover: image kindly supplied Shannon Stapleton/Reuters
Printed and bound in Great Britain by CPI Group (UK) Ltd, Croydon, CR0 4YY
Policy Press uses environmentally responsible print partners

FSC
www.fsc.org
MIX
Paper from responsible sources
FSC® C013604

"As a dedicated pro-choice activist Judith is best placed to write this informative and well-pitched analysis of issues related to defending abortion rights."

Kerry Abel, Chair of Abortion Rights, Britain's national pro-choice campaign

"Relevant, informative, engaging and necessary – this book is a crucial weapon in the battle for a woman's right to choose."

Saba Shiraz, student, University of West London

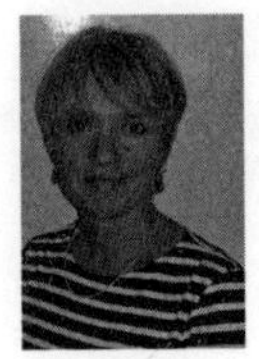

Judith Orr has decades of experience campaigning and writing on women's rights and abortion. She grew up in Northern Ireland where abortion is effectively illegal. She is an elected member of the executive committee of the national Abortion Rights campaign.

As a journalist, she reported from Cairo's Tahrir Square during the Egyptian Revolution, in particular highlighting the role of women in the struggle. She has written two previous books, *Marxism and Women's Liberation* and *Sexism and the System,* and has spoken on her work internationally including in Canada, Germany, Austria, South Korea, Ireland and Turkey.

For Esther Orr

Contents

List of abbreviations

ALRA	Abortion Law Reform Association
BBFC	British Board of Film Censors
BMA	British Medical Association
BPAS	British Pregnancy Advisory Service
CACB	Campaign Against the Corrie Bill
CGIL	Italian General Confederation of Labour (*Confederazione Generale Italiana del Lavoro*)
DFID	Department for International Development
FAB	Fight the Alton Bill
FN	Front National
FPA	Family Planning Association
GMC	General Medical Council
IFPA	Irish Family Planning Association
KRW	South Korean Won
NAC	National Abortion Campaign
NHS	National Health Service
NUS	National Union of Students
PTSD	Post Traumatic Stress Disorder
RCM	Royal College of Midwives
RCOG	Royal College of Obstetricians and Gynaecologists
SPUC	Society for the Protection of Unborn Children
SRE	Sex and relationships education
TUC	Trades Union Congress
UCL	University College London
WHO	World Health Organization

Acknowledgments

This book is partly a product of collective debate and campaigning on abortion rights with many people over many years. But I would like to thank a number of people for their specific help with this project including Kerry Abel (Chair of Abortion Rights) and Ann Henderson (Abortion Rights Committee in Scotland). Mary Brodbin, Emma Bircham, Anna Gluckstein, Jane Hardy, Amy Leather and Roddy Slorach read parts or all of earlier drafts and offered feedback and advice, for which I am very grateful. Of course, any errors in the final book are all my own work.

Annette Mackin transcribed many interviews, turning them around in superfast time even when the one or two I first mentioned turned out to be many more. An old friend whom I marched alongside over abortion rights as a student, Fiona Watson, also helped with transcriptions, delivering them across time zones. Yesong Lee translated the interview with Hyun-ju Lee. Many thanks to all of you.

I would also like to thank everyone at Policy Press, particularly my editor Victoria Pitman, as well as Shannon Kneis, Rebecca Tomlinson, Jess Mitchell and Kathryn King.

Most of all, I want to say how grateful I am to all the interviewees who gave their time so generously and shared their stories with me. I would also like to pay tribute to all those at Abortion Rights with whom I have worked over the years. Their tireless work has ensured the protection of abortion rights in Britain and continues to challenge the limitations on a woman's right to choose.

ONE

A choice moment

Never before had so many people, across so many borders, marched in unison for women's rights on a single day. 'Women's Marches' filled the streets of cities across the US, Britain and all over the world in support of reproductive rights on Donald Trump's first day as US President in January 2017. The sea of 'pussy hats' and witty homemade placards that marked this historic outpouring of anger and solidarity left no corner of the globe untouched.

The Trump presidency presents a new threat to gains of the past, and reducing reproductive rights is a central plank of his agenda. Trump and his Vice President Mike Pence made no secret of their desire to target abortion provision before their election victory. Pence had signed eight pieces of anti-abortion state legislation into law in four years as Governor of Indiana (Berg, 2016). Trump had talked of the need for 'some form of punishment' for women who have abortions. He had also claimed that if Hillary Clinton became president she would make it possible that, 'in the ninth month, you can take the baby and rip the baby out of the womb of the mother just prior to the birth of the baby'.[1] Like so many of Trump's lies, this was challenged in the aftermath of the debate. But it was too late to stop this lurid scenario – so beloved of the anti-abortion camp – reaching a television audience of 70 million people.

The photograph of Trump surrounded by men signing a new 'global gag' order on 23 January 2017 was symbolic of what this presidency means for abortion rights worldwide. The order denies federal funding to any international aid bodies who give advice about abortion services, let alone deliver them, including if they only use their own money for such work. Marie Stopes International estimates that as a result of Trump's ruling, funding cuts to their services could result in 6.5 million unintended pregnancies, 2.1 million unsafe abortions and 21,700 maternal deaths. It will also prevent contraception reaching 1.5 million women every year.[2] In response, an alliance of countries committed funds to try to fill the gap left by the removal of US contributions. International aid is already affected by the political bias of rich individual 'benefactors'. Billionaire Melinda Gates, for example, will not allow any of the Gates' donations to international aid agencies to be used for abortion services – although she does not dictate what such agencies do with their other funding, and she opposes the global gag (Furedi, 2016).

For those who depend on aid agencies for all of their health care, including access to contraception and abortion services, the global gag may be a death sentence. Making abortion illegal, unaffordable or inaccessible doesn't make abortion go away; it kills women. To be more specific, it kills poor women. The World Health Organization (WHO) figures speak for themselves. The WHO calculates that 56 million induced (safe and unsafe) abortions occurred worldwide each year between 2010 and 2014.[3] Over 21.6 million women experience an unsafe abortion worldwide each year, 18.5 million of which occur in developing countries (Cook et al., 2014). The consequences of these unsafe abortions are stark: 47,000 women die from complications annually, meaning that deaths due to unsafe abortions constitute close to 13% of all maternal deaths.[4]

With abortion rights under attack in the US, the richest country in the world, the poorest there also suffer the most serious consequences. As Dr Willie Parker, an abortion care provider in Mississippi's single abortion clinic and a clinic in Alabama, said: 'The harsh laws restricting access to abortion here mean that disproportionately the women being denied access to abortion care are women of colour and poor women' (see interview with Dr Willie Parker in Voices from the frontline at the back of this book). The very basis for legal abortion in the US, the historic 1973 Supreme Court decision known as Roe v Wade, is under threat. Individual US states can impose limits on access and severely restrict provision, but Roe v Wade still protects the fundamental right to abortion. Pence has declared he and Trump would see 'Roe v. Wade consigned to the ash heap of history where it belongs'.[5] Trump has declared that it will 'automatically' be overturned because he will appoint 'pro-life' justices to any vacancies in the Court.[6] Indeed, Trump's first appointee to the Supreme Court was Judge Neil Gorsuch. The US Physicians for Reproductive Health decried the nomination, saying Gorsuch 'has a record of undermining health care access for women and is not someone who will reject medically unnecessary restrictions that endanger women'.[7] The anti-abortion Right now has a potential majority in future votes on cases concerning abortion provision.

Pence himself spoke at the annual anti-abortion 'March for Life' within a week of becoming vice president. He was the highest ranking Republican politician ever to take part in person. He made it clear in his speech that he was appearing with Trump's blessing, saying Trump 'actually asked me to be here today'.[8] Trump has also opened an assault on funding for Planned Parenthood – the main provider of family planning advice and services in the US – and Obama's Affordable Care Act. Among the many consequences of this is that women, mainly poor and working class women, could face losing guarantees of birth control coverage.[9] Trump has also filled the health department and his administration with anti-abortion appointees. Some even oppose contraception; these include Katy Talento, now a health-care adviser on his Domestic Policy Council, who claims that taking the contraceptive pill causes abortions and infertility. Talento has written to women whose doctor prescribed them the pill, asking: 'Did she tell you that the longer you stay on the Pill, the more likely you are to ruin your uterus for baby-hosting altogether?'[10] Abortion access and Roe v Wade were already facing regular challenges by state legislatures even before Trump became president (Grimes & Brandon, 2014; Pollitt, 2015). These challenges have now been given a dangerous new impetus and a powerful means to impose them.

The election of Donald Trump is a pivotal moment in a new war on abortion rights. It has given confidence to right-wing political forces and the anti-abortion lobby everywhere. The question of abortion is in the spotlight internationally to a degree that has not been seen for decades. But rather than intimidating the pro-choice side, a new generation has been galvanised to join the struggle to defend a woman's right to choose. This book will look at the latest assaults on women's reproductive rights and what they mean. It will also put the current struggles in the context of the long history of attempts to control women's bodies and their fertility, and within the wider experience of women's oppression.

Backstreet or safe abortion

Presidential orders, restrictive laws or dogmatic benefactors do not stop abortions happening. They just ensure women are forced to take more desperate and dangerous measures to end an unwanted pregnancy. Abortions happen every day, everywhere, whatever the law, whatever the official provision or lack of it and whatever the moral judgements society lays down on women. Internationally, the WHO estimates that, between 2010 and 2014, one quarter of all pregnancies ended in induced abortions.[11]

There is a host of reasons why a woman might be faced with an unintended pregnancy. Contraception can fail; people forget to use it, or use it incorrectly. Women can become pregnant after rape. Older women may have had reason to believe they were no longer fertile. So, there are a multitude of reasons women have abortions. Having sex does not equate to wanting to have a child. A pregnant woman may feel she is too old, or too young, to have a child. She may already have children and not want another. She may discover that she is carrying a foetus with a fatal abnormality. She may have wanted to get pregnant but changed circumstances – perhaps experiencing bereavement, separation or domestic violence – led her to decide she no longer wants a child. She may simply feel unable to afford it, or that it's not the right time, or she may have decided she never wants to have children. Yet despite abortion being such a common part of women's reproductive lives, it is surrounded by taboos, social stigma, legal constraints and mythical dangers. One in three adult women of childbearing age in Britain and the US will have an abortion[12], yet many women don't even tell family and friends, let alone talk about it in public.

Ending an unwanted pregnancy should be a simple technical or medical issue – safe and straightforward methods of carrying out abortions have been available for some time. In Chapter Three, we will see that the vast majority of abortions in Britain are carried out at a very early stage in pregnancy. These are generally medical abortions, in which women take two tablets: mifepristone and misoprostol. Mifepristone is taken first, which blocks the hormone progesterone and causes the lining of the uterus to break down. Then, usually a day or so later, the woman puts misoprostol tablets under her tongue or between her gum and cheek, or in some instances into her vagina, to dissolve. These make the womb contract, causing cramping, and over a period of hours the pregnancy is terminated much like an early miscarriage. These tablets are used all over the world, and in countries where abortion is illegal many women buy them online. The WHO includes both drugs in its list of 'Essential Medicines'.[13]

The other most common form of abortion is vacuum aspiration. This can be carried out with a local or general anaesthetic and takes 5 to 10 minutes. It involves a tube being inserted through the cervix and into the womb, after which suction is applied extracting the contents of the womb. For abortions from around 15 weeks, a dilation and extraction is commonly used. After dilating the cervix, narrow forceps are inserted through the cervix and into the womb to extract the pregnancy. This too can be done with local or general anaesthetic and takes 10 to 20 minutes.

But these simple procedures are not treated like any other part of women's reproductive health care. Abortion is a social and political issue. Politicians, religious leaders and the 'moral' Right impose their views and judgements on women and their bodies and exercise their power against women's choice at every opportunity. As we will see, throughout history it is the poorest women who are most affected by such crackdowns. Women with money have always been able to access the safest abortion care available.

Church and state control of women's fertility

One longstanding slogan of the pro-choice movement is 'Not the Church, not the state, women must decide their fate'. State restrictions and religious dogma worldwide continue to deny women the right to make their own decisions about their own fertility. Birth control is sometimes used as a political tool. In some parts of the world this means barring abortions, and even in some cases access to contraception. In others, it means limiting women's right to have babies by encouraging abortions or imposing sterilisation. For example, in China the state imposed a one-child rule in 1979, replaced with a two-child rule in 2015, as a method of population control. This means millions of women have abortions even when they may want another baby. Richer women can pay a fine if they break the rules. Most women don't have that option, as the case of Feng Jianmei in 2012 showed. There was outrage when it was revealed that the 22-year-old had been taken by officials when pregnant with her second child and forced to go through an abortion seven months into her pregnancy. She and her husband could not afford to pay the fine for having a second child.[14] Forced abortions are illegal, but local officials – who were prosecuted in this case – are under pressure to deliver population control targets.

Japan also has a history of using fertility control as a method of population control (Okamoto, 2014). Since the end of the Second World War abortion has been easy to access, but this is now changing. Japan's government is worried about the decline in population exposed by a census in 2016. It wants to encourage a higher birthrate and is even offering women discounted egg freezing so they can try for children when they have established their career. But at each stage it is the needs of the national state that are shaping policy, not those of ordinary women and men.

Church leaders of many faiths subscribe to a vision of family life that fetishises motherhood as women's defining role. The Catholic Church has been the flagbearer for the anti-abortion cause, colluding with states in majority-Catholic countries to try to maintain legal bars on most if not all abortions. It upholds its hardline anti-abortion stance as part of unchanging religious doctrine and has backed and funded anti-abortion campaigns internationally. In the wake of revelations about the Church's cover-up of widespread clerical child abuse, senior Church figures have asserted that abortion is a worse sin. For example, in 2002, after revelations about the extent of child abuse by priests in Australia, Cardinal George Pell was denounced for claiming that 'abortion is a worse moral scandal than priests sexually abusing young people'.[15] The sentiment was repeated by another senior figure in the Vatican, Cardinal Antonio Canizares Llovera, in 2009, when the scandal of child abuse in Ireland was being uncovered.[16]

The Catholic Church also opposes the use of contraception, although where it is available contraception is widely used even in majority-Catholic countries. Church establishments' decrees do not always dictate what their members think or how they behave. A poll showed that 48% of Catholics and 33% of Evangelical Protestants in the US believed abortion should be legal in all or most cases.[17] In Britain, 9 out of 10 Catholics support the wide availability of contraception and 7 out of 10 believe women should have the right to an abortion.[18] But although religious dogma may not always be obeyed, it helps create and perpetuate the stigma and feelings of guilt and shame some women feel when they attempt to control their fertility. The Catholic Church is not alone in its use of religious doctrine to oppose abortion. Increasingly, the evangelical Christian Right, particularly in the US, is aggressively anti-abortion and has used this as a rallying call to push restrictive legislation and hostile picketing of abortion clinics.

Across Latin America, different national laws make all or most abortions illegal. This situation remained unchanged even at the height of the Zika virus in 2016. This affected pregnant women and led to at least 4,000 children being born with microcephaly, which causes a smaller head size as well as affecting the brain. Pope Francis declared that there might be dispensation for women to use contraception in the affected region, saying 'avoiding pregnancy is not an absolute evil' and might be 'the lesser evil'. But he also told the majority-Catholic populations that he ruled out any change in the Church's opposition to abortion, regardless of the distress faced by so many women. He repeated the assertion that abortion was a crime: 'It is killing one person to save another. It is what the mafia does … It is an absolute evil'.[19]

Despite the Pope's intervention, the website Women on Web, which aims to provide abortion services to women in countries where they are banned, reported a threefold increase in enquiries from the region at the height of the crisis. They included heartbreaking emails from women desperate to access abortion. One woman wrote:

> I dare to write you because I'm a resident in Colombia and here the Zika virus is a major problem, although the health authorities haven't recognised it … I want to ask for help because I'm overcome by fear that my baby will be born sick. I already have two girls and work long and hard as a single mother to provide for them. Life in Bogotá is difficult enough without being in charge of a sick child, especially with the health system so precarious in Colombia.

Dr Rebecca Gomperts is the Dutch founder of the organisations behind Women on Web and Women on Waves. She has pointed out that many women across Latin America do not have access to the internet, and also may not be able to read, so there will have been many more women with nowhere to turn.[20]

Turning back the clocks?

Mainstream conservative politicians often have a contradictory stance on abortion. Conservatives have historically seen the traditional family as an institution fundamental to maintaining social stability and cohesion. This view sees women's domestic childbearing role as central, and such politicians have been the most resistant to the changing reality of women's role in society. But they are torn between their desire for women to take responsibility for looking after the next generation and other dependents and their need for women in the workforce. Working women both contribute to the economy and help to provide for millions of families dependent on their income to survive, whether in couples or single-parent families. The alternative to women working outside the home is a greater dependence on the welfare state, which is under unprecedented attack by successive governments across Europe.

The imposition of austerity has led to severe cuts in public services, the jobs of those who provide them and welfare benefits. This has disproportionately affected working-class women, and has had an impact on reproductive choices. For example, in Britain, parents of children born since April 2017 only receive Child Tax Credit for two children, not any further children they might have. The only exception is if women can 'prove' a further child is a product of rape – a requirement that has been widely condemned. Isabelle Kerr, manager of the Glasgow Rape Crisis Centre, denounced the clause while giving evidence to a Lords Secondary Legislation Scrutiny Committee on its implications saying, 'This clause puts women and children in an untenable position. It also potentially puts women's lives, and the lives of their children, in danger'. [21]

Society's judgement is harshest on single parents, 86% of whom are women.[22] Since Tony Blair's 1997 government first cut benefits to single parents, attacks on welfare benefits – on which many single parents have to rely – have been relentless. A barrage of poisonous propaganda has often accompanied these attacks, using themes that we have seen replayed time and again around women's lives. But this ideology is not just about making examples of women judged to have transgressed; it is rooted in the desire for the state to avoid responsibility for the upbringing and welfare of the next generation. If you are a woman who does not need benefits, anything goes. There are no great public outcries about avoiding responsibility if a wealthy single woman employs round-the-clock nannies to look after her children – in fact, she is more likely to be coined a 'superwoman'.

Trump's ascendancy in the US has put right-wing populist politics on the world stage; yet his agenda is not unique. Such ideas have been gaining support across Europe, with ominous implications for women's reproductive rights. One common feature of the rise of this new wave of right-wing populism and Fascist-type parties is the promotion of traditional gender roles and opposition to women's rights in general and abortion rights in particular. Social issues such as abortion are seen as a useful way to whip up the electoral base of the Right. The former leader of the fascist Front National (FN) in France, Jean-Marie Le Pen (father of the current leader, Marine), has described abortion as 'anti-French genocide'.[23] Marine Le Pen has tried to rebrand the FN and soften its public image. But her niece Marion Maréchal-Le Pen, France's youngest MP when elected for the FN in 2012 aged 22, has been unequivocal. She opposes publicly funded family-planning clinics, saying they are 'peddling abortion as something that's run-of-the-mill'. She resigned from the FN after Marine Le Pen lost the presidential election in May 2017.[24] In Britain, the former leader of the UK Independence Party, Paul Nuttall, compared those who carry out abortions to mass murderers, writing in 2012: 'Killers such as Ian Brady and Ian Huntley have their "human rights" and did not face the death penalty for taking the lives of children. Who is to defend the unborn child faced with a death sentence?'[25] The issue of abortion is not going to go away. Wherever the populist far Right makes advances, attacks on abortion rights are a likely part of their package of assaults on the gains made in recent decades.

But as politicians try to launch new attacks on women's rights, they face resistance. In 2016, even before Trump won the US presidential election, tens of thousands had taken to the streets in unprecedented numbers in both Ireland and Poland to fight to defend and extend abortion rights. In Poland, this included a women's general strike on 3 October 2016 – 'Black Monday'. The protests blocked a socially conservative right-wing government from tearing up the few rights available to women under already repressive anti-abortion laws; this inspired moves for women's strikes in the US and Europe on 8 March 2017: International Women's Day. Similarly, on 24 September 2016, a demonstration of over 30,000 people in Dublin 'more than tripled the numbers from the year before, which itself had at least double the numbers from the year before that … the size of the crowd, its youth, enthusiasm and determination surpassed most people's expectations' (Halpin & O'Grady, 2016, p3). Mass protests in Spain, another majority-Catholic country, forced back an attack on the legal right to abortion in 2014. The attempted change would have outlawed almost all abortions. Women marched with the slogan 'My belly is mine', and polls showed majority support for the status quo that had been won in 2010, giving women the right to an abortion up to 14 weeks and in certain circumstances up to 22 weeks.

Across Asia, feminist groups in India, young women activists in Sri Lanka and campaigners in Pakistan are taking up the issue of reproductive rights for women in societies where, whatever the law, women are often denied real agency over their bodies. In South Korea, activists inspired by the revolt in Poland protested in October 2016 against plans to extend an already punitive anti-abortion law that threatened greater punishments for doctors carrying out abortions. As Korean activist Hyun-ju Lee explains: 'Abortion is still illegal in Korea. It is only allowed in very rare cases and even then women must obtain the consent from her male partner' (see interview with Hyun-ju Lee). A coalition of social organisations, Left groups and feminists in South Korea came together to oppose the new crackdown and demand a women's right to choose, saying: 'Women aren't wombs. They are people before they are mothers'.[26] Within weeks, the government was overwhelmed by mass protests challenging state corruption, and the new law was abandoned.

Women have shown they are sick of their bodies being used as political footballs. The new activism is in part a symptom of the renaissance in struggles challenging every aspect of women's oppression in recent years. A new generation of women has got organised. They have had enough of discrimination, of the commodification of their bodies, of sexist imagery and treatment and living as second-class citizens. They balk at the gaping mismatch between the reality of women's role in society today and backward-looking laws and ideology that seek to control their bodies. The fight for access to full reproductive rights is becoming a key part of what's driving this activism.

The scale and exuberance of the Women's Marches in January 2017 were a symbol of this new mood of resistance. In Britain, over 100,000 marched in London alone. This was not just a sign of solidarity with women in the US; this was a warning that any attempt to turn the clocks back on women's reproductive rights in Britain would be met with opposition. This was seen in the protests of pro-choice campaigns against the deal done by Tory Prime Minister Theresa May with the Democratic Unionist Party

(DUP) to ensure a majority after the snap election in June 2017. The DUP are vehemently anti-abortion and have been central to blocking abortion rights in Northern Ireland. For while it is right to protest the excesses of right-wing populists internationally, we also have to address the problems closer to home. Trump talked about punishing women for having abortions. This book will highlight the fact that this is already happening in one part of the UK. In Northern Ireland, as Chapter Two illustrates, a woman received a three-month suspended jail sentence in 2016 for giving herself an abortion.

Class, race and reproductive rights

Why do campaigners who support the right to abortion argue that they are pro-choice? First, whether or not to have an abortion is ultimately up to the woman who is pregnant – it is her choice. It shouldn't be politicians or doctors making decisions on her behalf; they are not the ones who are pregnant and who will ultimately have the responsibility for looking after any child that is born. Second, reproductive rights must cover all aspects of women's fertility – not only the right to abortion but also the right to have children and to bring them up in safe and supportive circumstances.

State-enforced sterilisations have not only been motivated by population numbers. They have often been targeted at minorities. For example, a family planning programme launched in Peru in 1995 saw over 272,000 women and 22,000 men from indigenous communities sterilised: 'There are accounts of people being coerced, forced by medical staff or sterilised without their knowledge while in hospital for another procedure'.[27] In the 1950s and 1960s, many African American women in the US were sterilised without their knowledge or consent; in Britain, Black women were disproportionally given long-term contraception such as Depo-Provera and encouraged to have abortions (Davis, 1981; Seal, 1990, p33).

US political activist Angela Davis pointed to the dangers in not understanding how race[28] and class shape women's reproductive choices:

> Birth control – individual choice, safe contraceptive methods, as well as abortions when necessary – is a fundamental prerequisite for the emancipation of women. Since the right of birth control is obviously advantageous to women of all classes and races, it would appear that even vastly dissimilar women's groups would have attempted to unite around the issue ... But in actuality, the historical record of this movement leaves much to be desired in the realm of challenges to racism and class exploitation. As for the abortion rights campaign itself, how could women of colour fail to grasp its urgency? They were far more familiar than their white sisters with the murderously clumsy scalpels of inept abortionists seeking profit in illegality. In New York, for instance, during several years preceding the decriminalisation of abortions in that state, some 80% of the deaths caused by illegal abortions involved Black and Puerto Rican women ... The campaign often failed to provide a voice for women who wanted the *right* to legal abortions while deploring the social conditions that prohibited them from bearing more children. (Davis, 1981, pp204–6)

Inclusive reproductive health care also means the need to recognise that trans men, and others who do not identify as women, may need to access services including birth control and abortion provision. Trans people face discrimination across many areas of life, and have increasingly forced the issue of the need to tackle and resist transphobia into the spotlight. A number of countries have required trans people to be sterilised before the gender they identify as can be legally recognised. France only dropped this law in 2016; Sweden's government is paying out compensation to at least 160 trans people who were forced to undergo this operation before the law there changed in 2013.[29] Such policies show why it is essential that sensitive reproductive health care – whether it is access to screening, contraception or abortion – is actively inclusive to everyone, however they identify.

These are the reasons the movement for full abortion rights is called 'pro-choice'. But choice in this context is not like a consumer selection in a shop or on a website – choosing a blue sweatshirt over a black one. It cannot be divorced from the oppressive structures, institutions and dominant ideas of the society in which the choice is being made. For example, the context of choice is affected if children born outside of marriage are deemed 'illegitimate', or if the women who bear them are stigmatised as 'loose' or immoral. The ability to make genuine choice is also shaped by the ability of women to be financially independent.

Reproductive rights have been, and continue to be, collectively fought for as part of a multitude of struggles opposing every expression of discrimination against women. Attitudes to abortion are closely bound up with the impact of class and society's views on gender roles, sexuality and the family. These same forces shape women's ability to make reproductive choices today, and in some cases threaten to roll back advances made decades ago. The next chapter will look at the impact on women of being denied choice. This includes the thousands of young women who gave birth outside of marriage and were forced into servitude in state and Church institutions in Britain and Ireland.

Women's liberation: asking too much?

Women are told we 'can't have it all' – as if wanting to be financially independent and have a secure home and perhaps children is really asking too much. It is as if we have to accept the idea that if you have a womb you'd better limit your expectations. Women's lives, their work and domestic arrangements are constantly a feature of public debate. Women are in a no-win position when it comes to their fertility. You are damned if you choose abortion, and society tells you being a mother is the height of your destiny. But if you do choose to have children you face discrimination, low pay and expensive childcare. Women who have children when they are young are vilified as irresponsible and financially penalised if they can't go out to work. Yet women are also criticised for having babies too late; for spending too much time building careers, and forgetting their ovaries and eggs are as old as them. The Italian government tried this tack in 2016 with a poster used to promote a new initiative to encourage women to have children, called 'Fertility Day'. The poster portrayed a photo of a woman holding an hourglass, with the words: 'Beauty knows no age. Fertility does'. They had to withdraw it after protests. Men are rarely stigmatised in the same way for late fatherhood. In fact, pensioner dads – such as rock musician and great grandfather Mick Jagger, who became a father for the eighth time aged 73 in 2016 – are celebrated for their virility.

One of original five demands of the Women's Liberation Movements in both Britain and the US was abortion on demand. The Abortion Act 1967 in Britain is 50 years old, yet women in Britain have still not achieved this right. Without this ability to control our fertility, women will never be able to play a full and equal role in society. Every woman must be able to choose what she does with her own body, including when or if to have a child. This is a fundamental right, which is why pro-choice activists increasingly frame the issue of abortion as one of human rights. A number of legal cases have been brought from across Ireland, for example, on the basis that being denied safe and legal abortion in the case of rape or incest is in contravention of human rights law.

This book is not a neutral account of these issues. It takes as a starting point the belief that every woman – regardless of race, class or nationality – has the right to full reproductive rights, including the ability to choose and access a safe, free, legal and prompt termination. Everyone has a unique life experience and set of circumstances, and the decision whether or not to bear a child is not an abstract policy matter that should be the plaything of politicians. It is the gut-wrenching realisation experienced by a woman when she finds she is pregnant and doesn't want to be. It must be a woman's right to choose what she does with her body – no one else's. It doesn't seem much to ask that every child should be a wanted child; indeed, it seems eminently rational. Yet today, the right to terminate an unwanted pregnancy is still controversial.

In a series of interviews that illustrate the reality of the issues this book addresses (see Voices from the frontline) we hear from people who have found themselves on the frontline of these battles. Women who have undergone backstreet or illegal abortions before 1967, doctors who provide abortion care in Britain today and want to see the law changed, and women who have campaigned for abortion rights across the decades are all included. Diane Munday, who was central to the campaign that helped win legal abortion through the Abortion Act 1967, will describe how her own illegal but safe abortion drove her to campaign for the right to choose for all women. Activists from both sides of the border in Ireland will talk about their experiences in fighting laws that deem abortion a crime and why they think the tide is finally turning in favour of change. Dr Willie Parker will reveal what it's like to provide abortion care in the southern states of the US today. He explains why he is dedicated to ensuring women can access abortion services despite current restrictions and the threat of more under Trump's presidency. Together these interviews, which were carried out by the author and will be quoted and referred to throughout the book, offer a diverse range of experiences. They bring home the human impact of restrictive laws and prejudice on women's reproductive rights. They make the case for change.

Structure of the book

This book will explore current debates about abortion rights and look at why they continue to be such a contested part of women's health care. Chapter Two will look at the impact of the current law on reproductive choice in the UK (where the Abortion Act 1967 doesn't extend to Northern Ireland), the Republic of Ireland (where abortion is effectively barred from the constitution) and Poland (where even very restricted rights to legal abortion are under threat). The chapter also discusses the impact of online services for women in countries where abortion is banned, and the problem of anti-abortion doctors citing conscientious objection to refuse to carry out terminations even where abortion is legal.

Chapter Three will point to evidence throughout history that trying to control fertility and avoid unwanted pregnancies are age-old problems because humans have sex for pleasure, not just procreation. Women have resorted to everything – from crocodile dung and lead pills to knitting needles and bleach – when determined to have an abortion. In fact, such is the extent of women's experience of ingesting compounds to terminate a pregnancy over thousands of years that it is the source of much modern knowledge of poisons (Jenkins, 1960; Widgery, 1975).

The Abortion Act 1967 was a tremendous achievement and profoundly affected millions of women's lives in Britain. In Chapter Four, we will hear from some of those who helped to achieve the passing of the legislation, as well as its impact. But 50 years on, we cannot simply celebrate the fact that women in Britain are no longer going to the backstreet. The Act was a compromise even in 1967; today, the law is an anachronism that is obstructing possibilities opened up by the latest medical advances. For example, sexual health doctor Jayne Kavanagh points to examples of the current law's negative impact on delivering care, arguing that 'decriminalising abortion is important for clinical and social progress' (see interview with Dr Jayne Kavanagh).

Chapter Five will look at the arguments, strategies and tactics of those who oppose abortion rights. It will expose the agenda they want to pursue and show how their activity helps create and sustain the stigma that surrounds abortion, even where it is legal. This is bound up with society's expectations of women's sexuality and what is seen as their traditional role in the family, as this chapter shows.

Chapter Six explores the roots of the ideology that has infused debates about women and abortion for centuries. It shows why abortion is regarded as the ultimate rejection of a women's natural purpose: it is bucking not only biology but also the ideology that tells us biology is our destiny. Challenging such prevailing ideas has always been part of the struggle for reproductive rights. However, Chapter Six will show that not all women experience the same controls and moral judgements. It will explore how public condemnation has been particularly virulent when it comes to the lives and choices of working-class and poor women, who have always been more severely policed than their middle-class and wealthier sisters. Working-class and Black and minority ethnic women have also found themselves routinely characterised as feckless, irresponsible and promiscuous. This book will show

how such prejudices were at the heart of eugenicist ideas that influenced the early birth control campaigns of the 19th and 20th centuries. But women have refused to be passive in the face of repression, even in the harshest circumstances, and their agency will be celebrated.

This book also charts the inspiring struggles of all those who have fought for a woman's right to choose – the women and men who have stood up for abortion rights whatever the political climate, who have marched, lobbied and helped individual women facing prosecution and social exclusion.

Finally, we will look to the future. Chapter Seven asks: what could abortion provision look like in the 21st century and how can we harness the latest technological and medical developments to best serve women's needs? Doctors on the frontline of provision will give their views on these questions. The different options open to women today will also be compared to the 1960s generation. The internet has often been described as the new backstreet, but this virtual backstreet is different from the literal one of the past. If women use reputable web sources, then they can access reliable abortion medication.

But even where women can access safe websites, why should they have to go underground to access health care? Why can't women in the 21st century access an abortion at a local doctor's surgery or clinic as easily as arranging a cervical smear or breast screening and as part of their general health-care provision? These are the questions that many people are asking today. It's clear that the battle for a women's right to choose is still one that will have to be hard fought. This book will argue that it's time we shed the legal and economic restraints on women's reproductive choices, as well as the stigma and moralism that still surround abortion. This struggle for reproductive rights, for the freedom to control our bodies, is central to the struggle for a different society – one in which women are not treated as second-class citizens.

TWO

A web of solidarity

There are many fronts in the battle for abortion rights: street protests, legal cases, working for better legislation and wider access, providing alternative abortion services and supporting women forced to travel to access care. This chapter will look at some of these fronts. It will start with the UK, where the law is a barrier to full access and even its benefits don't reach Northern Ireland. It will then look at the Republic of Ireland, where the fight is to remove an effective bar on abortion from the constitution, and Poland, where even the most minimal rights are under threat. It will also examine the impact of online services for women trapped within borders where abortion is banned, and barriers put up by oppositional doctors even where abortion is legal.

Britain

Abortion in Britain today has never been easier or safer. The use of pills for medical abortions has revolutionised abortion provision. Yet archaic laws and ideology still restrict women's ability to access the full benefits of medical advances. Successive polls show a majority in Britain support legal abortion. An Ipsos MORI poll in early 2016 found that Britain had the third most positive attitudes to abortion (after Sweden and France) out of 23 countries, with 62% saying a woman should be able to have an abortion 'if she decides she wants one'.[1] All the major trade unions in Britain support a woman's right to choose. The British federation of trade unions, the Trades Union Congress (TUC), organised Britain's biggest ever pro-choice demonstration in

1979 as part of a major campaign to defend the Abortion Act 1967. The campaigns within the women's movement, the trade unions and the Left to defend abortion rights will be explored in Chapter Five. But it is significant that the sheer scale of the 1979 TUC mobilisation knocked back the anti-abortionists for years.

Such a level of public support dissuades most mainstream anti-abortion campaigners from open calls to completely repeal the law and ban abortion. Instead, anti-abortion campaigns in Britain more often seek to undermine the law in increments. So this chapter will start by looking at abortion provision in Britain today: what's the law, what's the practice and what's the problem?

What's the law?

In England, Scotland and Wales, abortion rights are governed by the Abortion Act 1967. In England and Wales, this created exemptions under which doctors could legally carry out an abortion without being prosecuted under the Offences Against the Person Act 1861. The 1861 Act makes abortion illegal outside these specific conditions, with a punishment of 'penal servitude for life'.[2] This law from a century and a half ago is still the basis for abortion law today in England, Wales and Northern Ireland. The 1861 Act didn't cover Scotland, which used common law on abortion until 1967. The conditions laid down for abortion to be legal are that two doctors agree that:

> the pregnancy has not exceeded its 24th week and the continuance of the pregnancy would involve risk of injury to the physical or mental health of the pregnant woman or any existing children of her family, greater than if the pregnancy were terminated.

Doctors can also take into account 'the pregnant woman's actual or reasonably foreseeable environment'.

The only amendment made to the law since 1967 came in the Human Fertilisation and Embryology Act (1990), which set the time limit for abortions at 24 weeks – although it also lifted any time limit for certain circumstances, including where the continuance of the pregnancy would involve risk to the life of the pregnant woman greater than if the pregnancy were terminated. Exemptions from the 24-week limit also include where a termination is 'necessary to prevent grave permanent injury to the physical or mental health of the pregnant woman'; or 'there is substantial risk that if the child were born it would suffer from such physical or mental abnormalities as to be seriously handicapped'.

The Abortion Act 1967 was a triumph. It created conditions for legal abortion and has mainly been interpreted liberally, saving thousands of women's lives (Sheldon, 1997). Before 1967, the only option for many working-class and poor women was to go to the backstreet (coined the 'back alley' in the US) for an illegal and potentially dangerous abortion. This Act deserves to be celebrated and has to be defended against its critics who claim it went too far. As Chapter Four will explain, the Act originated as a Private Member's Bill moved by Liberal MP David Steel in 1966. When attacked by anti-abortion campaigners, Steel quotes a remark that the former Secretary-General of the British Medical Association (BMA), Dr John Marks, made in his retirement speech in 1992: 'Looking back over these 40 years, it seems to me that the event which has had the most beneficial effect on public health during that period was the passage of the Abortion Bill'.[3] Yet despite the very real advances made by the Act, it was flawed from its very inception. Compromises made in 1967 to ensure that it passed left a contradictory legacy, which means a women's right to choose is conditional and constrained.

What's the practice?

In 2016, 185,596 women resident in England and Wales had abortions; the figure for Scotland for the same period was 12,063. If you include non-residents the total number of abortions performed in Britain was 202,469.[4] The National Health Service (NHS) funded 98% of these, although two thirds were carried out in private clinics such as Marie Stopes and the British Pregnancy Advisory Service (BPAS).[5] One study gives a snapshot of the broad range of women who have abortions: 'In 2013, over half (53%) of women who had abortions were already mothers – a proportion that has been relatively constant for a decade. In 2013,

67% of women having abortions were either married/in a civil partnership or single, but with a partner' (BPAS, 2015, p56). As mentioned previously, the vast majority of abortions in Britain today are carried out at an early stage in pregnancy. Department of Health figures show that, in 2016, '92% of abortions were carried out at under 13 weeks gestation and 81% were carried out at under 10 weeks, which is slightly higher than in 2015 at 80%, and considerably higher than 2006 at 68%'. More than half are medical abortions, 62% – a proportion that is on the rise, and more than double the percentage in 2006. Less than 0.1% of abortions happen after 24 weeks, and only in the exceptional circumstances detailed earlier.

What's the problem?

The biggest problem is that Northern Ireland was excluded from the 1967 Act (discussed shortly). But even in Britain, legality doesn't guarantee abortion access. There has always been a postcode lottery; that is, your level of service depends on where you live. In Scotland, the NHS carries out almost all abortions, but will generally only provide them up to 18 weeks – a restriction that has no basis in law. Women needing terminations after that time must travel to England, where Scotland's NHS will pay the bill and refund travel if you know how to apply (Pearson, 2015).

Anti-abortion campaigners attempt to whip up moral panics, claiming there are too many abortions in Britain because getting an abortion is too straightforward. They want to put even more hurdles in the way of women accessing terminations. 'Is 197,659 abortions in Britain each year too many?' is really the wrong question. The right number of abortions is the number that is needed. Those that claim there are too many must answer the questions: which ones would you ban? Which woman would you tell, 'you are legally obliged to carry this pregnancy full term'? Before the Abortion Act 1967, no one really knew how many abortions took place in Britain and official figures consistently underestimated the figures. The take up of legal abortion services after the Act surprised those who had chosen to ignore the fact that women previously had to try to solve the problems of unwanted pregnancy themselves – in the backstreet. As for the accusation that getting an abortion is too easy, the reality is that women already face too many hurdles to access abortion care in Britain. If your own GP is anti-abortion, you have to find another. Contrary to the wails of the anti-abortion lobby, women do not have 'abortion on demand'. The decision whether a woman can have an abortion is still very much in the hands of doctors – a position locked in by the Abortion Act 1967.

Northern exposure: the politicisation of the law

Abortion law in Northern Ireland is as it was in Britain pre-1967: illegal under the 1861 law, with a few exceptions. These are that continuing the pregnancy would 'make the woman a physical or mental wreck'. This exception was created as a result of a court decision in 1938 called the Bourne Case after the doctor involved. Aleck Bourne was a leading gynaecologist who carried out an abortion on a 14-year-old who had suffered multiple rape by a group of soldiers. His defiance of the law provoked prosecution, and he hoped the case would set a precedent to allow legal abortion under certain conditions. He won, and his victory opened the way for a broader definition of legal abortions that still stands in Northern Ireland. An Act that allowed abortion to save a woman's life – the Infant Life (Preservation) Act 1929 – was only extended to Northern Ireland in 1945. But these exceptions are rarely invoked. In early 2017, a 21-year-old was prosecuted under the 1861 Act for 'procuring poisons' – abortion pills bought online – to end her pregnancy, even though she was suicidal.[6] The Standing Advisory Commission on Human Rights issued a public consultation document on the issue of abortion in June 1993, which stated that the legal situation in Northern Ireland was 'so uncertain that it violates the standards of international human rights law'.[7] In March 2016, the Northern Ireland executive published a new set of guidelines stating that abortion is only legal if a woman's life is at risk or there is a permanent or serious risk to her mental or physical health.[8]

The High Court in Northern Ireland ruled in November 2015 that the laws on abortion in Northern Ireland breached the

European Convention on Human Rights, specifically for women who had been raped or in cases of severe foetal abnormality.[9] Judge Justice Horner stated that abortion law in Northern Ireland was in breach of human rights and 'smacks of one law for the rich and one law for the poor'.[10] The Northern Ireland executive appealed the ruling and the Appeal Court overturned this judgement in June 2017. It rejected the view that denial of abortion rights in such cases was a breach of human rights. The Human Rights Commission was set to take the case to the Supreme Court. A vote to widen access in such cases was lost in Stormont in early 2016.[11] Doctors in Northern Ireland may recommend an abortion to women who discover that their foetus has a severe or fatal abnormality, but not actually offer one. In such cases, a woman's pregnancy may be too far advanced for a medical termination with pills, so women are forced to travel to a strange city and clinic in Britain – often at a time of great grief at the prospect of losing a wanted pregnancy – and, until a change in government policy in 2017, pay many hundreds of pounds for an abortion. Couples sometimes want to bury the remains back home, or want a post mortem examination to find out the cause of a fatal foetal abnormality and have been known to be left with no alternative but to carry them back in a picnic cool bag.[12] Women often travel back immediately after an abortion to avoid the costs of staying in England, which also has implications for follow-up care.

The Family Planning Association has estimated that approximately 2,000 women have travelled to England from Northern Ireland every year for abortions. Official statistics are always an underestimate as some women do not give their real address to protect their privacy. The latest figures for 2016 show a drop in that officially recorded number to 724, but a rise in the number of women buying pills to on the internet.[13] In fact the number of abortions carried out in Britain on non-residents from any country in 2016, 4,810, is the lowest of any year since 1969. This would indicate the wider impact that online access to pills is having internationally. Recent studies show how easy and safe using pills for a medical abortion can be if proper advice is followed. Research published in the *British Medical Journal* in May 2017 showed that 95% of women in Ireland in the study who had carried out a medical abortion at home using pills after consulting online 'telemedicine' reported a successful termination without any other medical intervention (Aiken et al, 2017).

Until the sudden climb down by the Tory government in June 2017 women from Northern Ireland not only had to travel to access a legal abortion, they also had to pay for it in a private clinic. In every other area of health care, women in Northern Ireland were treated as part of the UK within the NHS. They paid the same taxes and the same National Insurance; yet for almost 50 years they had been barred from accessing free legal abortions on the NHS in Britain and were often forced to pay high sums for a private termination on top of travel expenses; with each week's delay, the price of a termination rises. The announcement that women from Northern Ireland would be able to access free abortions on the NHS when they travelled to England was made on the day of the Queen's Speech following the 8 June General Election. The election result saw Theresa May lose the Tories' slim majority and make a controversial deal with the DUP to ensure the Queen's Speech passed. Opposition to the DUP deal had shone a spotlight on the issue of abortion and the dire situation for women in Northern Ireland. Wide support gathered for an amendment to allow women from Northern Ireland access to NHS abortions in England. Theresa May was so anxious to avoid a defeat she overturned a discriminatory practice, which had been defended by politicians for decades, in just a few hours. Soon both the Welsh and Scottish Assemblies followed suit and announced they too would provide NHS abortions to Northern Irish women. Only two weeks earlier the Secretary of State for Health had fought and won a case in the Supreme Court to defend his right to refuse women from Northern Ireland access to NHS abortions.

The case in question was brought by a young woman and her mother, known as 'A' and 'B'. 'A' was 15 years old when she went to England for an abortion in 2012 – a procedure that cost a total of £900. The Court agreed that the policy of denying Northern Irish women NHS-funded abortions in England was discriminatory and that the Secretary of State for Health had the power to overturn it. But the three-to-two decision stated that he had to 'respect' the devolved parliament and that to allow free abortions to women from Northern Ireland might lead to a 'near collapse of the edifice of devolved health services'.[14] Evidently the prospect of the 'near collapse' of the new Tory government became a more pressing concern for Theresa May.

The change in policy is a real victory, but the fight for women in Northern Ireland to have the right to free, legal and safe abortions at home continues. Some women may have health conditions that make travel difficult or even dangerous, for many the travel costs alone are prohibitive. In April 2016, only months after Judge Horner's original judgement and statement, a woman in Northern Ireland received a three-month suspended jail sentence after buying pills online to cause an abortion at 10 to 12 weeks of pregnancy. She was 19 at the time. She had tried to raise the money to travel to England to have what would have been a perfectly legal termination, but couldn't raise enough so bought pills online instead. Her housemates reported her to the police. She was punished not only because she was a woman with an unwanted pregnancy in a country where abortion is illegal but also because she was poor. In protest at the sentence, a number of pro-choice activists collectively went to police stations in Northern Ireland and handed themselves in, declaring that they had either taken or procured pills on the internet and so should also be prosecuted. One of the protesters was Goretti Horgan from Alliance for Choice, who declared she had helped at least 20 women procure abortion pills. She said:

> These pills have been available now for 10 years. Not only are none of us particularly worried about this, we have stood outside police stations reminding police we signed letters giving them our names and addresses. We want the law sorted on this … The law that makes it illegal for women to take these pills is 155 years old, before the light bulb was invented. (Gentleman, 2016)

The police declined to charge any of the activists. They obviously feared the bad publicity a well-organised campaign could generate – in contrast to the prosecution of an isolated young woman who simply tried to solve the problem of an unwanted pregnancy in the only way she was able.

Pro-choice campaigners have pointed to the hypocrisy of the British government deliberating on other countries' abortion restrictions while ignoring anti-abortion law in Northern Ireland:

> The Department for International Development (DFID), in a range of publications, has indicated that it considers safe and legal abortion a human right ... The DFID supports safe abortion on two grounds. First, it is a right. Women have the right to reproductive health choices. Second, it is necessary ... in a humane and just society that women and adolescent girls must have the right to make their own decisions about their sexual and reproductive wellbeing. (Quoted in Horgan and O'Connor, 2014, p40)

Public opinion in Northern Ireland in support of change is moving faster than the politicians and the establishment. An Amnesty International poll in September 2016 showed that almost 60% of people in Northern Ireland believe abortion should be decriminalised. When people were asked about women who were pregnant as a result of rape, or women carrying a foetus that could not survive outside the womb, support for the right to abortion went up to 75% (Amnesty International, 2016b).

Border controls

South of the border, the Republic of Ireland has a different legal situation. The Eighth Amendment of the Constitution of Ireland equates the life of a pregnant woman with an unborn foetus in law, effectively banning abortion. This means as soon as a woman becomes pregnant she loses the right to bodily autonomy. The law has led to a steady stream of women who have an unwanted pregnancy travelling, mostly to Britain, to access a legal abortion. From the ferry and trains to today's budget air travel, the trip is a well-worn path. The Irish Family Planning Association (IFPA) calculates that between January 1980 and December 2015, at least 165,438 women and girls travelled from the Republic of Ireland to access abortion services in Britain.[15] Again such figures are always an underestimate, as women may not give an Irish address to protect their privacy. The numbers of women travelling has recently slightly decreased. The IFPA has stated that in 2015, '3,451 women and girls provided addresses from the Republic of Ireland at abortion clinics in England and Wales, a decrease of 7.6 percent on 2014'. In reaction to the latest statistics, IFPA Chief Executive Niall Behan pointed out that the decrease did not necessarily mean fewer women were seeking abortions: 'While it is impossible to quantify the extent of their use, abortion pills accessed online have had a significant impact on the decline in the number of women in Ireland seeking abortion services in the UK'.[16]

Pressure is building for fundamental change in Ireland. There is a sense that a critical moment has been reached in the fight for liberalisation of the law. Some activists point to the stunning victory in the 2015 referendum, legalising equal marriage for same-sex couples, as proof of how Ireland has changed. Increasingly, people are willing to openly state they have travelled to get an abortion, seeing silence as allowing the Irish state to turn its back on the problem. Some making the journey to England for an abortion have live tweeted their experience and attendance at an abortion clinic in order to make public what is so often a secret event.[17]

The tens of thousands who marched in Dublin in September 2016 are the most visible evidence of the latest struggle. They are part of a growing and broad campaign calling for the repeal of the Eighth Amendment of the Constitution. More than 70 groups make up the umbrella organisation Coalition to Repeal the Eighth Amendment, 'including women's rights and reproductive rights groups, civil and health rights advocates, trade unions and left-wing political parties' (Halpin and O'Grady, 2016, p16). The Secretary of the Coalition, Sinéad Kennedy, points out that 'collectively it represents about a million and a half people' (see interview with Sinéad Kennedy). The movement has been coined a 'new Rising for full rights for all citizens' because 2016 was the 100th anniversary of the Easter Rising against British rule. The Irish government tried to pacify the movement by setting up a Citizens' Assembly to discuss and make recommendations about abortion law. This was made up of 99 citizens and a judge as Chair, who listened to submissions from all sides. There were so many submissions about abortion they had to devote an extra weekend to the subject. At the end of the process in April 2017, the 99 citizens of the Assembly made history when a majority voted for abortion law to be changed in Ireland and for abortion to be available on request up to 12 weeks, as well as a number of other recommendations that would enable a woman's right to choose. A full referendum would still be needed to make such changes, but the result was a massive success for the pro-choice side who will step up pressure for a change in the law to be put to the vote.

The Eighth Amendment is a result of a referendum in 1983, when 67% supported the call to change the constitution to effectively ban abortion. But the evidence is that public opinion has shifted markedly since then. An Amnesty International poll in February 2016 found that the 'overwhelming majority of people in Ireland want access to abortion expanded (87%) and abortion decriminalised (72%) … on many questions, there were progressive views on abortion across all regions and socio-economic groups' (Amnesty International, 2016a). The poll also found that 66% consider it 'hypocritical' that the constitution bans abortion in Ireland but allows women to travel abroad for one. As many as 72% believe that forcing women to travel for abortions unfairly discriminates against those who cannot afford to or are unable to travel, with 55% describing Ireland's abortion laws as 'cruel and inhumane'. As for the impact of Catholicism, the survey showed that '82% of those who consider themselves religious agreed that their religious views should not be imposed on others' (Amnesty International, 2016a).

Melisa Halpin and Peadar O'Grady (2016) analysed the trends in public opinion from a number of polls over time, and wrote: 'we see support of 64% … rising … to 74% respectively for repeal … with opposition to repeal falling from 25% … to 18%'. This demonstration of the declining hold of the Church is a product of women's changed expectations of their lives. But the Church's credibility has also been seriously undermined by the exposure of enormous scandals of child abuse and cover-up over many decades. Such scandals include the cruel treatment of women who became pregnant when they were not married and were put in 'mother and baby homes'. The Church faces contradictory internal pressures about how to maintain influence. On the one hand are those who favour accommodation to the expanding expectations of women, many of whom are central to the Church's congregations. On the other are those who want to maintain a more dogmatic approach. The Pope's announcement in November 2016 that he was giving priests the power to 'forgive' women who had had abortions is a sign of these tensions. Until then, only bishops could forgive an abortion, still described in the announcement as 'grave sin'.[18]

Challenges to laws on abortion in Ireland have in part been stimulated by reaction to high-profile cases. In 1984, the case of Ann Lovett, a 15-year-old in Granard, Co Longford, caused an outcry. She died after giving birth alone to a baby who didn't survive at the town's grotto to the Virgin Mary. At the time, women were barred from even receiving information on abortion, as well as from travelling to another country to have one. This was the situation until a referendum changed the constitution in 1992 so that the Eighth Amendment couldn't be used to deny women the right to travel. This change was after the shocking case known as the 'X case' in 1992, when a 13-year-old girl who had suffered rape was stopped from travelling to England for an abortion. The Irish Supreme Court overturned the bar on her travel, but the fury the case provoked meant the momentum for at least minimal change in the law was unstoppable.

In 2012, Savita Halappanavar, an Indian national living in Ireland, died after being denied a lifesaving abortion in a hospital in Galway when she fell ill at 17 weeks of pregnancy. A midwife attending her said she could not be given abortion because 'Ireland is a Catholic country'. When news of her death broke, vigils and protests took place across Ireland and internationally. The legal response led to the scrapping of the infamous Offences Against the Person Act 1861, a relic of British imperialist rule. In its place came the current law, the Protection of Life During

Pregnancy Act 2013, which allowed abortion when a woman's life is at risk or where there is a risk of suicide. But lengthy 'guidelines' published by the government shortly after the law was put in place were revealing.[19] They showed the Act would rarely be allowed to be interpreted in a way that would permit women, even in the exceptional circumstances described, to access legal abortion. In fact, the IFPA described the guidelines as appearing 'more restrictive than the Act'. The guidelines begin by reiterating that abortion is a criminal offence, and go on to describe the labyrinth of hurdles any woman would have to go through to be allowed to terminate her pregnancy.

To access an abortion under the law, a woman may face between three and seven different doctors and psychiatrists to judge whether an abortion is justified. Research by *The Irish Times* found that one third of all psychiatrists in Ireland rejected the view that a woman should be granted an abortion if she is suicidal. This means that, in practice, the law offers no protection for even the most vulnerable women (O'Regan, 2013). This was proved by yet another appalling case in 2014. A young refugee in Ireland who had been raped in her own country was refused an abortion at eight weeks of pregnancy, even though she was reportedly suicidal. She went on hunger strike in desperation, but she was medically force fed and underwent a legally imposed caesarean without her consent at 25 weeks. The baby was taken into care.

These cases are the public ones; the tragedies resulting from sometimes the most extreme circumstances. They rightly cause loud and public outcry. But at the other end of the scale are the women who every single day make the journey across the Irish Sea. They go through the tough scrabble for money and booking flights, and on return have to fabricate excuses for being away from work and face the fear of health complications that might lead to questioning. All because they are deemed criminals for wanting to exercise their reproductive rights. Ireland has largely ignored international pressure to change its stance. The United Nations Human Rights Council declared that Ireland needed to lift its ban on abortion as part of its Universal Periodic Review in May 2016. Of the 19 recommendations made, Ireland accepted only one: 'a recommendation by Switzerland that the government engage with all the relevant stakeholders in determining whether the legal framework surrounding abortion could be broadened' (Fitzgerald, 2016). This was a minimal shift from the position in 2011, when Ireland had rejected all such recommendations.

Poland

Another European country whose laws force women to travel across borders to access abortion is Poland. Formerly part of the Eastern Bloc, Poland's laws on abortion were tightened more than once in the early 1990s after the fall of the Communist regime. Since then they have been among the most restrictive in Europe, only allowing abortion in rare and very specific circumstances: where the woman's life is in danger; where there is a risk of serious and irreversible damage to the foetus or where the pregnancy is a result of rape or incest. This latter condition has to be verified by a prosecutor. This means the vast majority of abortions that take place in Poland, even without any new restrictions, are illegal. Poland has a population of 38.5 million, yet only 1,000 to 2,000 legal terminations are recorded every year.[20] This compares to the 197,659 abortions in 2016 in Britain, with its population of just over 63 million. Some estimate that the number of illegal abortions in Poland could be as many as 150,000.[21]

In reality, so many doctors refuse to conduct even legal abortions, citing conscientious objection, that the ability to access a legal abortion is even more difficult than the law's conditions would indicate. Leading pro-choice activist and Director of the Federation for Women and Family Planning, Krystyna Kacpura, said her organisation hears of 'at least two or three such cases every day' (Kacpura, 2016b). She points out the hypocrisy of such doctors claiming conscientious objection as their reason for not carrying out legal procedures, because 'some doctors make this objection in their work at public hospitals while continuing to provide abortions at high prices in their private practice' (Kacpura, 2016b). What makes this situation even harder for women is the fact that contraception is expensive and sometimes hard to access. The morning after pill is available only by prescription, and a report in 2012 showed that a number of Polish doctors (and, increasingly, pharmacies) were using the cover of conscientious objection to justify their refusal to prescribe or stock even this (Kacpura et al., 2013).

With a far-Right government and the support of the Catholic Church, Polish women have few options but to go outside Poland; (for example, to Germany and the Czech Republic) if they find themselves with an unwanted pregnancy. The most recent attacks on even these limited abortion rights in Poland were not the first, but what was different was the defiant response they provoked. Hundreds of women and men walked out of Polish churches when priests read out the Catholic Church's support for the new legislation in April 2016.[22] Video clips of examples of this public rejection of the dominant religious institution in Poland went viral. But the strike and demonstrations on 'Black Monday' – when an estimated 100,000 people took part in pro-choice demonstrations across Poland including in Gdansk, Lodz, Wroclaw and Krakow – marked a watershed. Many who didn't strike wore black in solidarity with the protest, in which placards declared: 'My body, my choice', 'Fuck off fanatics' and 'Girls will overthrow the government' (Zebrowski, 2016).

The government did a U-turn within days, although a new and only slightly less draconian amendment was quickly composed, provoking yet more protests. Jarosław Gowin – Poland's Deputy Prime Minister and member of the ruling far-Right party, Law and Justice – said the protests had 'caused us to think and taught us humility'.[23] The draft law would have made it as difficult to get an abortion as in the Vatican or Malta, which have the most restrictive abortion laws in Europe. Opposition was so widespread that even the Catholic Church eventually backed away from the new law. It apparently finally balked at the clause that would have punished women who had undergone an illegal abortion. Kacpura (2016a) wrote that women 'make up the majority of the people who attend mass and give money', and the Church therefore couldn't afford to totally alienate them.

The trade union movement in Poland supported the pro-choice protests, including Poland's largest single union the Polish Teachers' Union (*Związek Nauczycielstwa Polskiego*) and the All-Poland Alliance of Trade Unions (*Ogólnopolskie Porozumienie*

Związków Zawodowych) federation. The mass mobilisations may have opened the potential to not only push back further restrictions but also challenge the pitiful legal provision women currently face. The Federation for Women and Family Planning reported that more people visited the organisation's office in June and July 2016 than in the previous 25 years (Kacpura, 2016b). This is a sign that increasing numbers of women are no longer willing to tolerate being forced to travel outside of Poland to access an abortion.

Conscientious objection

The issue of conscientious objection by health-care staff can have serious consequences for the availability of reproductive health care, even where abortion is legal. Of course, no woman would want to be treated by a hostile doctor who opposed the procedure she needed. But alongside the hypocrisy described in Poland is evidence of the deadly impact it can have elsewhere. For example, pregnant woman Valentina Milluzzo died in October 2016 in a Sicilian hospital after anti-abortion doctors refused her a termination. This was after she had gone into septic shock when one of the twins she was carrying died in the womb. Her death – in an obstetrics and gynaecology hospital in a country where abortion has been legal since 1978 – is a warning of how conscientious objection can undermine women's legal rights. In Sicily, 87.6% of gynaecologists refuse to perform the procedure, citing conscientious objection.

Research by pro-choice Italian doctor Silvana Agatone found that of over 10,000 gynaecologists in Italy, only 1,200 performed abortions.[24] She and many other pro-choice doctors are nearing retirement, and she worries about the rise in the numbers of young doctors claiming conscientious objection. In some regions women cannot find anyone prepared to perform abortions. In response, the Italian Association for Demographic Education sends pro-choice doctors weekly to parts of the country where women could not otherwise have an abortion (Pianigiani, 2016). For example, once a week doctors travel from Milan or Rome to Ascoli Piceno in east-central Italy to perform abortions in the city hospital, where there is not a single gynaecologist who will perform them.[25] This mirrors the situation in parts of the US, where pro-choice doctors travel from Chicago to the Southern states to carry out abortions when few or no other doctors in those states will provide them.[26]

Penalty fines for women found to have obtained an illegal abortion in Italy have increased from €50 to €10,000. Doctors report that the number of what are recorded as 'miscarriages' is rising because more women are having illegal abortions. Dr Agatone told *The Guardian* that the increased fines mean women fear seeking treatment: 'Now if a woman risks being denounced for an illegal abortion, she will stay at home even if she is not well. This is very dangerous'.[27] Italy's biggest trade union, the Italian General Confederation of Labour (*Confederazione Generale Italiana del Lavoro*; CGIL), filed a petition on the issue to the Council of Europe in 2013. The resulting unanimous judgement published in 2016 stated that Italy 'was violating women's right to health' (European Court of Human Rights, 2016).[28]

Doctors in Britain can also use conscientious objection to refuse to carry out abortions. This provision was built into the Abortion Act 1967 following lobbying by the medical profession. Two Glasgow midwives lost a case in the Supreme Court in 2014 when they tried to expand the law. They wanted to avoid even being involved with staff caring for women who were having an abortion (Brooks, 2014). One Marie Stopes study in 2007 found that 20% of GPs described themselves as 'anti-abortion', although not all of these refuse to refer women for abortions. Marie Stopes estimates that around 10% of GPs in Britain exercise conscientious objection (Marie Stopes, 2007).

There is worrying evidence that a growing number of younger doctors are refusing to take part in abortions (Strickland, 2011). The Royal College of Obstetricians and Gynaecologists stated almost 10 years ago that it was aware of a 'slow but growing problem of trainees opting out of training in the termination of pregnancy and is therefore concerned about the abortion service of the future'(RCOG, 2007). This may be caused by the stigma that still surrounds abortion, meaning it is not a prestigious speciality. It may also be a result, as abortion care provider Dr Tracey Masters indicates, of the separation and 'exceptionalising' of abortion from other aspects of women's health care (see interview with Dr Tracey Masters). But it may also reflect that abortion is not as appreciated as a vital lifesaving health provision by generations who have no experience or memory of the suffering and deaths caused by backstreet abortions.

Internet providers

Women seeking abortion services across the world have harnessed every possible means to overcome the legal and practical hurdles put in front of them. Today, that includes drones, ships carrying containers fitted out as medical suites and – most significantly – online prescribing. There has been an explosion in the alternative provision of abortion services to women internationally where abortion is illegal or difficult to access. For the majority of working-class women, many of whom already have children and jobs and bills to pay, the time and money it takes to travel to access a legal abortion can be prohibitive. The opportunity to use the internet to buy abortion pills has opened up new possibilities. Even women in countries where abortion is legal sometimes try to buy pills online if access to standard abortion services is denied or difficult. Buying abortion pills online does leave women open to being sold ineffective or even dangerous medical treatments; two safe and recommended websites are womenonweb.org and womenhelp.org. Women on Web lists many of the sites to be avoided, but buying pills from reputable websites is incomparably safer than the old backstreet (see Chapter Three).[29] In some places, access to online services has been absorbed into the mainstream of medical care. For example, women in Australia and in British Columbia in Canada can be prescribed abortion pills after an online consultation with a doctor, who then sends the pills by post.[30]

It is tough enough for women today, but imagine the situation for women in the past, who had to travel to access a legal abortion before the days of the internet or mobile phones. They had to find the numbers of abortion clinics in phone directories in phone boxes; Irish campaigner Goretti Horgan recalls Dublin city libraries removing the *Yellow Pages* phone directories because they contained numbers for abortion clinics.[31] Phone calls in Ireland had to be connected by operators who could listen in, when it was illegal to even pass on information on abortion. Ann Rossiter, an activist who herself had an illegal backstreet abortion, describes how they invented a code name for abortion – 'Imelda' – so they could 'fox the telephone operators who would snitch on you in a local area where everyone knew everybody, and more about you than you knew about yourself' (see interview with Ann Rossiter).

Where these services act in place of legal provision, buying pills online has been a lifesaver for women – despite the danger that they might accidently use a disreputable site. A recent study of women in Ireland accessing pills for a medical abortion from Women on Web found that 94% expressed gratitude that they were able to access abortion medication online (Aiken et al., 2016). One woman said:

> There is no way I could have afforded to travel to England, pay for the procedure, stay in a hotel, and have someone there to support me. Thanks to this service, I was able to have a safe abortion in an environment where I felt comfortable and with my partner there to support me. (Aiken et al., 2016)

The question of resources is central. As the same study pointed out, the legal situation in Ireland is creating 'a stark health inequity: women with financial and social resources can access offshore termination of pregnancy, while women who lack such resources cannot' (Aiken et al., 2016). Women on Web grew out of Dr Gomperts' original Women on Waves project, featured in the documentary Vessel.[32] She and fellow campaigners had the idea that they could use international maritime law to offer abortions to women in countries where it was illegal. They took a Dutch ship – governed by Dutch law, in which abortion is legal – and moored 12 miles off the coast of countries such as Ireland, Portugal and Poland. As they were in international waters, doctors aboard could legally carry out abortions. They faced opposition from authorities – in one instance, when they arrived near Portugal the government sent warships to block access.[33] But even when denied the ability to carry out abortions, their actions raised the profile of unjust abortion laws.

The power to help many more women was opened up by the ability to prescribe abortion pills online. It's been calculated that 5,650 women used Women on Web's 'telemedicine' service between January 2010 and 31 December 2015. Research found that 97% of women 'felt they made the right choice and 98% would recommend it to others in a similar situation' (Aiken et al., 2016). But even just buying pills online isn't that simple – if you live in the Republic of Ireland, you risk your package being confiscated. Irish customs officers seized over 1,017 packets of abortion pills in 2014, up from 653 in 2011. Now, Women on Web (who send pills in the required official packing) no longer posts pills to addresses in the Republic of Ireland. Women have to make other arrangements. Some have pills sent to a friend elsewhere, who forwards them after repacking them in a plain parcel. Others have them sent to an address in Northern Ireland and travel to pick them up. Yet even this route is threatened by a clampdown as police gained search warrants to search the premises of two pro-choice activists looking for 'drugs or instruments to cause abortion' on International Women's Day in 2017.[34] The next chapter will demonstrate how self-organisation to provide abortion services has long been a feature of women's campaigns for reproductive rights. As safe abortion procedures became available, but denied to women because of the law, women and men risked prosecution to help women get abortions or carry them out themselves. For example, when feminist writer Simone de Beauvoir joined other high-profile women in France to call for legal abortion in 1971, she signed a collective statement saying they had all had abortions and let activists use her flat for an illegal abortion network (Schneir, 1995).

One of the best-organised collective responses to illegality internationally was the Jane Project in Chicago in the early 1970s (Kaplan, 1997). This impressive underground network used the generic name 'Jane' as the code, just as the name 'Imelda' was used in Ireland. It directed and accompanied women to doctors who performed abortions in hotel rooms, initially with the women blindfolded to protect the doctors' identity. The group then went on to employ a doctor on a salary to carry out abortions in volunteers' homes, so it could charge what it thought women could afford and not turn any away. The volunteers sat in during the abortions, and gradually helped to carry them out. When, after a year, they discovered that the 'doctor' was in fact not medically qualified, they trained themselves to carry out terminations. Sympathetic local doctors trained volunteers in the safest procedures and provided medical backup for complications. As one Jane volunteer remembered, 'By the late summer of 1971, the blindfolds were gone, and so was the man' (Fried, 1990). In the years leading up to the legalisation of abortion in the US, as many as 300 women a week depended on this single informal self-help service. In all, it carried out 11,000 abortions between 1969 and 1973 (Gordon, 1990).

The ingenuity and solidarity that marks the attempts to get around the law and support women is inspiring. But women's rights should not have to rely on alternative provision of health care because of legal, economic or any other hurdles. Women's rights cannot be left to the whims of those who have never had to walk in the shoes of the people they judge. In the words of 1930s abortion rights campaigner Stella Browne, 'what should be a normal integral part of modern medicine and surgery is forced into the category of purchasable contraband' (quoted in Rowbotham, 1977, p112). This is as true today as it was almost a century ago.

THREE

Abortion: as old as humanity

Women have actively attempted to control their fertility for thousands of years. Anti-abortionists try to tell us that abortion is unnatural and abhorrent; in fact, it has been a necessary and accepted aspect of women's lives throughout history. From the earliest nomadic societies that could only sustain as many children as adults could physically carry to modern capitalism, women have used whatever means available to them to separate sex from procreation (Cashdan, 1985). It was only when the earliest horticultural and agricultural human societies began building more settled communities that bringing up more children became a possibility. For a time, increased numbers of children were also a premium for settled groups, because they created more hands to tend the land (Harman, 1999). Such changes helped enable a greater capacity to produce food, and for the first time a surplus over and above daily needs could be generated. All this had profound implications for future human societies over thousands of years, including the development of hierarchies, classes and elites for the first time (Flannery and Marcus, 2012). This process also began to form the basis of the exclusion of women to the domestic sphere (Empson, 2014). Some form of women's oppression has been a feature of every class society that followed.

The evidence shows that whatever the economic system, state of scientific knowledge or law, and however dangerous or limited their options, women have tried to end unwanted pregnancies (Mclaren, 1984; Shorter, 1984). Almost three thousand years ago in ancient Egypt, women were mixing a paste of fermented crocodile faeces or applying honey to their vaginas as contraceptives (Fryer, 1965; Draper, 1972, p60). This advice, alongside recipes for abortifacients (substances that cause an abortion), was found on scraps of ancient documents called the Kahun Gynaecological Papyrus, after the ancient town in whose ruins they were discovered; these shed light on what people knew about human biology and how they tried to control it. In fact, the documents are copies of even older medical writings showing that women had been experimenting with substances to control fertility from even earlier times. Many of the compounds and rituals associated with contraception and abortion reflected superstitious or magical ideas. But people used them because many of the plants, resins and other natural ingredients would have had a real effect. For example, the use of some plants such as acacia leaves and date palm keeps reoccurring over several millennia, and they have been shown to contain ingredients that are proven to curtail fertility (Riddle, 1992).

A plant called the Chaste Tree was referred to in many ancient Egyptian and Greek texts for its anti-fertility properties. Taking extracts of it with the herb pennyroyal – a form of mint – was said to bring on an abortion (Riddle, 1992). Oils and products of the Chaste Tree are still marketed today to regularise periods and balance hormonal changes in women. Evidence of attempts at both contraception and abortion was also well documented in ancient Roman society (Dowsing, 2000). One 2nd-century writer on gynaecology describes prescriptions, including one 'which expels a foetus of three months without any difficulty' using plants that will make a woman vomit or will act as a laxative. Roman governments even had to institute laws and cash incentives to ensure citizens had many children (Riddle, 1992).

Class divisions existed in these societies and cultures over thousands of years, so women were not a homogenous group. A minority of women in the Ancient World could hold high status – they could own property, divorce and become powerful 'priestesses' (Harman, 1999). Such women would have been able to use the most advanced medicinal remedies and physicians of the time. Their children would have been important inheritors of wealth and power. Slavery in ancient Rome meant some women owned slaves or could employ servants or wet nurses to care for every aspect of their children's needs. But slaves, male and female, were just another piece of property and any children born to them would, in turn, become the property of the slaveowner. The experience of childbirth and ability to control fertility for such women was very different to that of their owners.

Some of today's opponents of abortion use a phrase in the ancient Hippocratic Oath as evidence that doctors should not carry out abortions. The oath comes from the Greek physician of the same name who lived in the 5th century BC, and doctors still take it today. But even in Hippocrates' own time, the oath was not interpreted as barring abortion. The specific phrase in the oath warns against using a 'destructive' pessary for an abortion, seen as a dangerous method at the time. No such judgement is made about ingesting plants and herb drinks and compounds, which was common and accepted practice. Many methods of aborting were dangerous and were simply about inflicting violent shocks to the woman's body to end a pregnancy. In 1960, anthropologist George Devereux reported on studies of methods of terminating unwanted pregnancy in more than three hundred pre-industrial societies worldwide. He gives accounts of women climbing a rope and then jumping, or being buried up to their waists, or having hot stones or even hot ashes placed on their bellies. Some societies used some form of obstetric manipulation. He also reports the Inuit of South Sound using sharp objects – for example, seal or walrus ribs, sometimes covered in seal skin – to terminate a pregnancy (Devereux, 1960).

What is striking is that across the historical evidence and right back to the earliest written records there is a common theme of advice, shared knowledge and skills being reproduced about how to avoid or end unwanted pregnancies. Some of the recurring ancient ingredients such as pennyroyal, myrrh, tansy and thyme are still being mentioned in the Middle Ages, and pop up on different continents across the globe over hundreds of years (Mclaren, 1984; Riddle, 1992; Koblitz, 2014). In fact, these herbal substances were so effective that they were sought after until the modern day. In some public gardens in Europe, rue and savin bushes, originally used in Roman times, had to be put behind glass or fenced off because of their popularity with women desperate to abort as late as the 19th century (Shorter, 1984).

The sometimes thin but ultimately unbroken thread – from the earliest evidence of fertility control through to the Middle Ages – was enabled in part by translations of Arabic text into Latin in the Middle Ages. European cultures were catching up with developments that had taken place long before in the East, where some of the world's greatest advances in medicine took place. Historian John Riddle (1992, p127) shows that, among the earliest Muslim medical writers, 'the evidence of continuous usages of oral contraceptives and early stage abortifacients is abundant'.

The Middle Ages

> Burdened with children and landlords' rent;
> What they can put aside from what they make spinning they spend on housing,
> Also on milk and meal to make porridge with
> To sate their children who cry out for food
> And they themselves also suffer much hunger,
> And woe in wintertime, and waking up nights
> To rise on the bedside to rock the cradle,
> Also to card and comb wool, to patch and to wash,
> To rub flax and reel yarn and to peel rushes
> That it is pity to describe or show in rhyme
> The woe of these women who live in huts.
> (Layland and Economou,1996, p820)

This extract of a 14th-century poem by William Layland described the conditions for poor women in the medieval era. The Middle Ages saw the Church in ascendancy and controlling every aspect of society; monarchs were viewed as being anointed by God. The towering cathedrals of the period were the physical expression of the Church's dominance and built to instil awe and fear. The Church's all-pervading power was channelled through the hierarchies of the state to the feudal lords. These owned serfs and controlled the lives and the work of mass of the population, 90% of whom across Europe lived on the land. Oppressive laws and penalties were inflicted on the poorest sections of society to ensure their subservience, all justified by ideology that deemed this hierarchy as natural and God-given. Women came under particular scrutiny (Rowbotham, 1977); their lives, sexuality and fertility were a constant target of censure from 'church fathers and monks'; such regular condemnations of abortion and contraception have been interpreted as signs of the widespread use of these practices (McLaren, 1984).

Women's lives were constrained in every way. They were expected to remain virgins until they were married; sex in marriage was the only acceptable sexual activity, and this had only one purpose – procreation. Women across society had to submit in all matters to the male head of the family. Women who were part of the Royal Court or a lord's retinue had many of the comforts of the time, with the best available diet and a leisured life with servants and medical attendants, but they were still under the control of the 'master' of the household. Peasant women were supposed to accept a life of constant childbearing once they had married. While childbirth was a risk for all women, for poor women in the worst living conditions it was hazardous. Women depended on local 'wise women', who acted as informal midwives and purveyed a mix of superstition and folklore with practical knowledge of childbirth, potions and compounds that could be used as abortifacients or contraceptives.

The rich folk knowledge that such women built up about women's bodies, childbirth and pregnancy was threatened with the rise of medicine as a university-trained profession practised mainly by men. Male doctors often shunned 'women's health' and left it to local communities to look after themselves, which meant that many never learned about the numerous birth control agents being used. John Riddle writes: 'Renaissance writers knew less about birth control than did their medieval, Islamic and classical forerunners' (1992, p157). But although such folk knowledge did decline, it never completely disappeared. As late as 1886, a dictionary of plant names states (wrongly, but significantly nevertheless) that savin/juniper 'derived its name from its "being able to save a young woman from shame"' (Riddle, 1997, p240). The reference to 'shame' is telling and an example of the rise of censorious attitudes to women's sexuality. These are part of the history of the stigma that came to be associated with women who refused to accept that constant childbearing was the automatic consequence of being sexually active.

The authorship of written records and medical texts from the Middle Ages is in the main dominated by men, because women were often denied access to the educational opportunities developing within universities and the academy. One of the few female written sources gives some insight into what ordinary people knew and used for fertility control in Europe during this period. Hildegard of Bingen was an abbess in a German convent, and among her many other achievements she wrote on science and medicine. Unlike male scholars of her time, she did not reference ancient texts; instead, much of her knowledge was gleaned from observing what people living around the convent cultivated and how they used different plants and herbs. Her writings are full of ingredients that act on fertility; for example, she describes how oleaster can cause an abortion, and she makes the first written reference to tansy as an abortifacient (Riddle, 1992).

Many of these ancient ingredients had powerful effects on pregnancy, labour pains and bleeding. Some were simply a form of poison, the use of which had to be carefully measured to avoid taking a lethal dose. Folk knowledge and experience was always vital, which was why so many women in the past relied on the advice of local 'wise women' – if you didn't know how to prepare compounds, oils or teas made with these herbs, moulds and plants, you were at risk of taking a dose that could be fatally poisonous or have no effect whatsoever. Yet such women and their skills were seen as defying the power of the Church and establishment to control women's lives, and many suffered persecution. This culminated in the murderous moral panic that swept through parts of Europe for several hundred years from the 16th century, when as many as 50,000 women were murdered after being branded 'witches'. These 'witch hunts' and the killing spree they ignited created a climate of fear for women challenging society's constraints in any way. At least 200 women were convicted of being witches in England's eastern counties alone in the 1640s, and although the last execution for witchcraft in Britain took place in 1685 the law remained on the books for another 50 years (Harman, 1999).

Industrial Revolution

The Industrial Revolution tore up the old ways and propelled millions into new factories and industrial centres from the 1760s. In Britain, the focus of this account, peasants were forced off land they had worked for centuries by enclosures and poverty. The hardship they endured when thrust into the new factory production was unimaginable. The transition from a feudal, mainly rural society to the capitalist system we know today was not a peaceful one. It involved a revolution of economic relations that led to a complete upheaval of political structures and dominant ideology. The institution of parliament now challenged the once all-powerful monarchy and all the old certainties were gone. The extended peasant family was effectively destroyed and the newly formed working class found itself in overcrowded insanitary living conditions in sprawling city slums. These living conditions were chronicled in factory inspectors' reports, political commentaries, agitational pamphlets and the fiction of authors including Charles Dickens and Elizabeth Gaskell. Gaskell's *North and South* was based in the fictional town of Milton and modelled on Manchester, where she lived in the early 19th century. It was a compelling portrayal of the toll of the dangerous and dirty conditions on whole families who worked in the cotton mills.

In the real factories, women, men and children found themselves working long hours in gruesome conditions to earn enough to survive. What did this mean for women's reproductive choices? For women in the toughest manual jobs, it was a major feat to successfully carry a healthy pregnancy to full term. Many pregnancies ended in miscarriage, stillbirth or babies who died in infanthood. Investigations into working conditions found women giving birth on the factory floor because if they didn't go into work they would not be paid. As Friedrich Engels described in 1845 in his powerful account *The Condition of the Working Class in England,* an overheard exchange revealed much about the position of working women when they had just given birth:

> If these women are not obliged to resume work within two weeks, they are thankful, and count themselves fortunate. Many come back to the factory after eight, and even after three to four days, to

> resume full work. I once heard a manufacturer ask an overlooker: 'Is so and so not back yet'? 'How long since she was confined'. 'A week'. 'She might surely have been back long ago. That one over there only stays three days'. Naturally, fear of being discharged, dread of starvation drives her to the factory in spite of her weakness, in defiance of her pain. (Engels, 1973, pp175–6)

When women returned after childbirth to the factory, where they worked for 13 or more hours a day, their children were left with others and often sedated to keep them from crying of hunger. Women were desperate to avoid constant childbearing, yet effective contraception was still not accessible to most people. Early contraceptive sheaths had existed from the 16th century. They were made from many materials, including sheep intestine and leather and linen tied on with ribbon, but they were an option only for the wealthy (Knight, 1977). Most people still only had the options of withdrawal and the rhythm method, which was often misunderstood (Bland, 2002). But even when condoms began to be mass produced and more widely available after 1844, when the new method 'vulcanisation' created more elastic rubber, the cost meant they were still not generally affordable to many poor and working-class people.

Abortion was an everyday reality as women tried to avoid constant childbearing, and conditions even pushed women to infanticide as a last resort when all else failed. In Lionel Rose's classic work on the subject, he describes how some midwives who delivered stillborns were 'valued for their "churchyard luck"' (Rose, 1986, p88). One doctor observed in 1870 that 'the number of infants who left this world on washing days was remarkable' (Rose, 1986, p89). Coroners' records as late as the 1920s show that it was 'not uncommon to find the remains of newborn infants stuffed up chimneys or buried under floorboards' (Dyhouse, 2013, p97). It is hard to imagine the desperate circumstances that would lead to a mother leaving a newborn baby to die. It is also impossible to calculate how many babies were stillborn because of the wide use of abortifacients that failed. In such circumstances women might have hidden the body for fear of being prosecuted. A law that was on the books from 1624 to 1803 decreed that an unmarried woman found with a dead child was –uniquely in the law – assumed guilty of infanticide unless she could prove otherwise (Rose, 1986). The punishment was the death penalty.

The huge changes brought by the Industrial Revolution meant the world of the midwife's kitchen garden, with its medicinal plants and herbs, was left in the past. The new pills, poisons and chemicals that became accessible were what women reached for as abortifacients. People lived in such dire conditions that some commentators thought the family as an institution would not survive among workers. Workers' labour was essential to the new expanding industries, but the establishment regarded their lives and behaviour as 'unruly', ungodly and a threat to a stable and productive society (Pinchbeck, 1977). The employers, political establishment and the Church were intent on imposing order on the growing working class.

Imposing order meant also trying to crack down on women's attempts to control their fertility. Avoiding and ending unwanted pregnancies was a fundamental challenge to the Church's teachings, which insisted sex was not for pleasure but for making families. Women who in different conditions might have wanted to have children took their fertility into their own hands, even at risk to their lives. The alternative – to carry a pregnancy and bring up children in immiseration – was too bleak.

Crime and punishment

The first major state action to bar abortion was bundled into the Malicious Shooting and Stabbing Act 1803, often called the Ellenborough Act after the Lord Chief Justice who proposed it. It included a clause on abortion alongside other assorted crimes, such as wilfully setting fire 'to any house, barn, granary, hop oast, malthouse, stable'. It took away the assumption of guilt for women accused of infanticide and treated it like any other crime of murder. But it also made abortion before 'quickening' – when the foetus was felt to move – illegal for the first time. The distinction of the moment of quickening was an old one and significant because the pregnant woman herself defined it, not a doctor or any other person. Even the Church for a time didn't treat ending a pregnancy in the first weeks as seriously as after quickening. But the new law meant that someone carrying out an abortion before quickening was punishable by transportation, whipping or imprisonment. The punishment for abortions after quickening was death (Greenwood & Young, 1976). This was later amended to take away the death penalty and the distinction between before and after quickening, until the Offences Against the Person Act 1861 outlawed all abortions, abortionists and – for the first time – women having an abortion. This Act was exported throughout the British Empire from Ireland to Australia, and is the one that's still on the books in most of the UK today.

The new laws were part of a drive to deter women from using home remedies and self-help in the community and instead to come under the authority of a medical establishment growing in power. These were contradictory developments. Women had been forced into a situation where they had to rely on other women in the community for advice and intervention around contraception. The lack of official medical intervention should not be romanticised. Because of the great dangers of self-medicating, many working-class women in the 19th century and into the 20th century would have gone to a doctor if they could have afforded to, and if they believed they would have received sympathetic advice. Even those women who did seek a doctor's advice were often refused help (Knight, 1977).

Yet regardless of what the Church or state decreed, abortion – which had been common throughout the 18th century – continued to be so during the 19th. Even after 1803, most women still believed it was legal to terminate a pregnancy up to quickening (Rose, 1986). In fact, some historians (Knight, 1977) claim it was the most used form of contraception for working-class women. The Catholic Church asserted a change in its own view of the significance of quickening in 1869, when Pope Pius IX decreed that 'ensoulment', when the soul was understood to enter a foetus, began right from conception (Riddle, 1992, p162). This made all abortions at any time a crime in the eyes of the Church as well as the state. Yet officials were heard to despair about the number of women who still had no idea they were breaking the law when they ended an unwanted pregnancy.This was a misconception that was widely held well into the 20th century (Knight, 1977). Women's actions were hard to police, as abortifacients such as lead pills and gunpowder mixed in margarine or water in which nails and pennies had been soaked were easy to obtain.

From the mid-19th century, Britain saw the start of a sharp decline in family size. This decline was no accident; most researchers agree it was partly due to a large rise in abortions, despite draconian laws. Prosecutions doubled in the first decade of the 20th century, and then doubled again in the following two decades (Lewis, 1984). Abortion became so common that unscrupulous businesses saw it as a way to make a profit, and a large commercial industry grew. This was mainly aimed at better-off women, and because of its illegality it was couched in euphemisms. A typical advert ran: 'Ladies only, The Lady Montrose miraculous tabules are positively unequalled for all female ailments.The most obstinate obstructions, Irregularities, etc of the female system are removed in a few doses' (Lewis, 1984, p17). Thousands of such products were sold in pharmacies, herbalists and through mail order. They were at best ineffective, at worst dangerous, but certainly commonplace. Another advertising slogan was:'Many ladies like to keep a box handy'(Knight, 1977, p61), making it clear women used such remedies regularly and not just in a rare emergency. In fact, one observer commented that some women never took chances and 'drenched themselves with "violent purgatives" monthly as matter of course' (Holdsworth, 1988, p98).

The number of women who bought these products was brought home by the infamous Chrimes brothers' blackmail case in 1899.The three brothers sold 'female remedies' through newspaper adverts.They then sent blackmail letters to 10,000 of their clients, claiming a legal case had been brought against them and they would only avoid arrest if they send a postal order for two guineas. This was a significant sum, even for middle-class women. Such was the fear of exposure that £800 had already been sent in the few days before the police found the brothers and arrested them (Knight, 1977; Francombe, 1984).

Class and fertility

Women of the upper and middle classes lived in different worlds to the majority of women, who endured multiple pregnancies when contraception was unaffordable and abortifacients didn't work. Wealthy women's bodies and fertility were indeed controlled by laws and morality, but as in the past they had access to the safest and most effective contraception and abortion procedures of the day. When birth control campaigner Margaret Sanger worked as a nurse in New York at the start of the 20th century working-class women remarked to her that, 'it's the rich that know the tricks ... while we have all the kids'(Alaimo, 2000, p112). As the law bore down on working-class women, the ideology surrounding women's role in society was wielded to impose a model of the ideal family on workers. This reflected a middle-class Victorian vision, with men as the breadwinners and women the chaste homemakers. This model was used as a way of keeping women (and men) in line, and moral judgement was passed on those who did not conform (Gordon, 1990). In fact, the very same system imposing this model was actually making it impossible for the mass of workers to have the choice to enjoy any sort of personal or private life. The ideal family simply wasn't an option for most workers. Class shaped the dominant perceptions of sexuality in society. Sexual freedom for working-class women was, and still is, judged as dangerous and needing policing. Women were told they should be conforming to their defined role of upholding the 'sanctity' of the family and marriage, with no recognition of the harsh reality of their existence.

A snapshot of working-class women's lives is portrayed in a 1915 document called *Maternity*, which makes chilling reading. It is a set of interviews with women published by the Women's Cooperative Guild. To understand the drive to dangerous abortions, it's necessary to appreciate the suffering and sheer physical burden of motherhood and childbirth when you are undernourished, overworked and full of dread. One woman describes how her baby 'was literally torn from me' (p116). Another said: 'I really feel that women are really worse off than beasts' (p48). One woman reported knowing three others who had died after taking abortifacients (p169). Another friend who already had seven children survived after she took a drug to terminate a pregnancy. When they met in the street, the woman told her: 'I will not have any more by him, and I should not have cared if I had died'(p169).

Doctors worried about publicising dangerous side effects of specific abortifacients in case it led to even more women using them. For example, a number of articles in the *British Medical Journal* at the turn of the last century gave accounts of a rise in deaths due to lead poisoning – but unlike outbreaks due to lead in the water, these only affected women. The doctors discovered that women had learned that working in factories that used lead caused miscarriages, and so they began using it to cause abortions. The doctors wrote about how the use of lead compounds spread through a geographical area around South Yorkshire, in particular across big 'manufacturing populations' (Hall and Ransom, 1906). They concluded that knowledge about the effect of lead on pregnancy was passed by word of mouth, as it took over a decade to spread to three or four counties from the first examples. Yet even as the use of lead as an abortifacient grew, doctors still worried about publishing concerns: 'there is a fear that publication might tend to spread the evil, instead of reducing it' (Hall and Ransom, 1906).

But as the establishment and some campaigners looked on with disapproval, paternalism or horror at the lengths to which women would go to avoid or end pregnancies, working-class women organised themselves. It's interesting to note that in some regions and industrial sectors smaller families were more common. There have been many debates about what the basis was for smaller families, and not everyone agrees on the reasons behind the changes (Mclaren, 1978; Roberts, 1999). One study in Bradford showed the birthrate fell after the introduction of legislation that restricted child labour in 1877 (Fryer, 1965). Other studies show that families were smaller in areas where women had paid employment (Gittins, 1982). One doctor in 1906 talked of experts' 'alarm' at the rise of the use of abortifacients 'in our industrial centres' (Rose, 1986 p134). Another doctor told a 19th-century parliamentary committee: 'where individuals are congregated in factories I conceive that means preventative of impregnation are more likely to be generally known and practised by young persons'. (Barker and Drake, 1982, p153).

In her 1914 report *England North of the Humber*, eugenicist birth control campaigner Ethel Elderton showed how common abortion was – particularly in urban working-class areas. Her report confirms that, where women were able to collectively meet and talk, they shared their experiences. Advice as to what might bring on a 'late' period was an important part of this. Collective factory work offered both economic incentive and opportunity to access the most effective methods from co-workers. This continued in the decades that followed. Abortion rights campaigner Alice Jenkins describes one factory in 1938 in which women workers paid into an 'abortion club' to take care of themselves if they needed to get help to terminate a pregnancy (Hall, 2005). The procedures used were described by Betty Brown, a worker in a jam factory in Grimsby in the 1930s:

> If you got pregnant you was told by some old woman to go to the chemist and get one shilling's worth of Penny Royal or Bitter Apple and take it with some gin. It used to make you very sick. They used to say keep taking it and you will have a mis. If you was very desperate they used to say use a knitting needle but always have a bottle of Lysol in because of blood poisoning and you died within hours if this happened. (Humphries, 1989, p78)

The same woman described how her friend died after following advice to move a mattress to the bottom of the stairs and jump from the top step (Humphries, 1989, p78). Working-class women did their best to look after each other, and local women were still often relied on for advice and practical help in carrying out abortions right up to the change in law in 1967. Such abortionists were often seen not as malevolent but as important allies. Women often refused to name their abortionist in court, or even when dying from a botched termination. When a court sentenced a woman named 'Mrs Lee' to five years' penal servitude in 1930, the *Gloucester Journal* reported 'a big demonstration' in her support and observed that protesters roundly booed those who gave evidence against her when they saw them at a window of the court building, shouting: 'Come down you dogs' (Francombe, 1984, pp71–2).

These abortionists were not seen as preying on women, but rather as helping them solve a problem. Moya Woodside (1966) interviewed 44 women in HM Prison Holloway who had been sentenced for carrying out illegal abortions during the 1960s. She found that all the women were or had been married, and the majority had children of their own. Several reported the support they had received from women they 'helped', including one who had been sent 'flowers and presents by her workmates before she went for trial' (Woodside, 1966, p37). But there were abortionists, female and male, who took advantage of women's situation to make money – and worse. The notorious serial killer John Christie of 10 Rillington Place posed as an abortionist and was eventually hung for the murder of several women in 1953, three years after an innocent man was hung for one of the murders. However, because of the taboo over abortion in the 1950s, the fact that Christie was practising as an abortionist was largely hidden as a component of the case at the time (Jones and Pemberton, 2014).

Working-class and poor women who couldn't afford to gamble on the semi-commercial remedies only had the backstreet. But those in the labour movement were in a position to organise collectively. For example, before the First World War, working-class women in Rotherhithe, southeast London organised birth control classes, which were still going in the 1920s (Fryer, 1965). Their class organisation gave them collective strength, and they had the greatest stake in the fight to change the law.

New struggles

The start of the 20th century was characterised by resistance and revolt. Women in the Suffragette movement mobilised to demand the vote, militant workers' struggles created what was coined 'the Great Unrest' and British rule in Ireland was challenged by a growing movement for independence (Dangerfield, 1997). These political and industrial struggles were not distinct from women's fight to control their fertility; they influenced, and were in turn influenced by, that ongoing fight. Historian Stephen Brooke (2013) places the struggle for birth control at the heart of class politics and socialist organisation from the turn of the last century. Women were at the centre of the industrial struggles of the 'New Unionism' in the 1880s, which saw the organisation of workers across many previously non-unionised industries. The Match Women of the East End of London, often coined the Matchgirls' strike, led the way in 1880, with a magnificent strike that exposed both their appalling working conditions and their ability to challenge them (Raw, 2011). We will see that these struggles, and the experience of mass employment of millions of women in two world wars, had a lasting impact. Women's expectations of their lives were expanded, and they increasingly questioned their position in society.

The first organised birth control movements began in the late 19th and early 20th centuries. But arguments for birth control have never taken place in a vacuum, and can play a contradictory role. Birth control can be imposed and shaped by racism and anti-working-class prejudice, or chosen as self-autonomy and genuine alleviation of suffering. That's why reproductive rights must always start with the right of women to have choice and autonomy over their own bodies. Sometimes a lack of understanding the limits of genuine choice has led to campaigners criticising women's behaviour. For example, it led some birth control activists at the turn of the last century to complain that working-class women seemed to prefer abortion to preventative measures. This was at a time when many advocates of birth control actively opposed abortion. But the reality was less about preference than the limited choices shaped by class and ideology that poorer women faced. Contraception was not accessible or affordable. In contrast, abortion was only needed if you actually fell pregnant. Also, for many working-class women contraception actually had more of a sense of 'immorality' associated with it: using it implied you had a lot of sex just for fun. So some women would have avoided it because of its associations with prostitution and 'loose' women – in their eyes, if they used contraception they wouldn't be seen as 'respectable'(Brookes, 2013). This anxiety was not unfounded; for example, one MP in the 1930s condemned birth control as 'the knowledge of the prostitute' (Jenkins, 1960, p49).

The majority of early campaigners were not driven by a desire to enable women to be more sexually liberated. Historian Lucy Bland (2002) has written about the development of birth control organisations from the late 1870s, starting with the launch of the Malthusian League, which saw convincing the educated classes of the need for population control as its priority rather than offering practical advice or agitating among the working class. The reactionary eugenicist and Malthusian views that shaped this early movement were based on the ideas of Thomas Robert Malthus, although many in the Malthusian League did not subscribe to all his ideas. Malthus had argued that the world's population was destined to grow exponentially and so outstrip resources, which were only growing arithmetically. He claimed this meant population numbers had to be controlled. Eugenics fed into the belief that certain people or sections of society were genetically superior and should be encouraged to 'breed', while those deemed inferior – often by reason of their class or race – should not be allowed to reproduce. Such eugenicist ideas became the mainstream in the US and Western Europe during the early 20th century. For example, it was eugenic legislation in Britain that condemned women who gave birth outside marriage into institutions; in the US, eugenic legislation led to the previously mentioned state-ordered sterilisations of poor, Black and Native American women, which carried on well into the 1970s (Schoen, 2005; Nelson, 2003).

The attitudes of many middle-class campaigners to poor and working-class women were often infused with at best paternalistic views about their poverty and bad conditions and at worst open bigotry. Some high-profile campaigners for access to birth control, including Marie Stopes in Britain and Margaret Sanger in the US, sometimes expressed the prejudices of the time. For example, Stopes complained that 'society allows the diseased, the racially negligent, the thriftless, the careless, the feeble minded, the very lowest and worst members of the community, to produce innumerable tens of thousands of stunted warped and inferior infants' (in Weeks, 1981, p190). Of course, this view has long been rejected by the services that bear the

Marie Stopes name, which are at the forefront of supportive and sympathetic reproductive health care for all women.

Even for campaigners without such attitudes, liberation for women was rarely the central issue. Their concerns were more often dominated by the desire to lessen the burden of incessant childbearing on poor women. Yet simply not having money was not enough to explain why women wanted to control their fertility. As one campaigner put it, 'even if we lived in Buckingham Palace we would not want a new baby every year' (Brookes, 2013, p86). Far from rejecting women's traditional role as mothers and family builders, this ideal was regularly emphasised by many birth-control campaigners, who argued that access to birth control made for better mothers of fewer children.

In contrast, some activists did see access to birth control as part of a wider struggle for a more egalitarian society, such as Bolshevik Alexandra Kollontai in Russia, who wrote that access to safe abortion was 'women's fundamental democratic right' (Porter, 2013, p333). In Britain, there was always a minority who saw the issue as one of women's liberation. Lucy Bland has pointed to the League members who approached birth control from a feminist point of view and those who supported getting information out to working-class women and men. At the time, even just distributing material on birth control to a working-class audience was regarded as dangerous; campaigners Annie Besant and Charles Bradlaugh had been taken to court in 1877 for publishing such information (Fryer, 1965). Alice Vickery, one of the League members to whom Bland points, was a defence witness in their case. She was Britain's first women chemist, and one of only five women in Britain to be awarded a medical degree in 1880 (Bland, 2002). Canadian-born Stella Browne, a founder of the Communist Party in Britain, also argued that 'birth control is women's crucial effort at self determination' (Hall, 2011). Another campaigner who argued that birth control was about emancipating women and their sexuality was Malthusian League member Jane Hume Clapperton. She stated her position in a pamphlet published in 1900, titled *What do Women Want?* She commented that 'sex-intercourse that is voluntary, pleasurable, healthful … is of comparatively rare occurrence' (Bland, 2002, p211). Historian Sheila Rowbotham has also written of the women who challenged the eugenicists; she points to the contradictions of the women who saw the issue as purely one of individual freedom. For example, she quotes socialist feminist Teresa Billington-Greig saying in 1915 that an unwanted baby was a 'terrible infringement of the personal rights of the mother' (Rowbotham, 2010, p102). In contrast, Rowbotham points out that women rooted in the collective tradition of the labour movement and the Left saw reproduction as both 'an individual and a social matter' that could not be extracted from the question of class (Rowbotham, 2010, p102).

The political establishment resisted women's tremendous struggle for the vote with everything at its disposal. Suffragettes were arrested, imprisoned and force fed when they went on hunger strike in protest (Foot, 2012). The suffrage movement encompassed the high-profile Suffragettes such as Emmeline Pankhurst and her daughters Christabel and Sylvia, as well as thousands of working women who wanted the vote both for themselves and for fellow male workers, who were also denied it. Sylvia became disillusioned with the tactics of the campaign led by her mother and sister, and went to east London to organise among poor and working women. There, she set up a maternity clinic and nursery, among other services. At the same time, working-class suffragists such as former mill worker Selina Cooper also saw the vote as part of wider struggles of their whole class, including the fight for access to birth control (Liddington and Norris, 2000).

The outbreak of the First World War pushed these struggles to the sidelines. Most upper-class Suffragettes supported the war drive, while many working-class suffragists opposed the war because they saw that ordinary people suffered the worst consequences. One such suffrage campaigner was socialist Hannah Mitchell, who declared: 'War in the main is a struggle for power, territory or trade, to be fought by the workers, who are always the losers'(Klein, 1997, p27). But whatever the views on the war, it played a material role in transforming women's lives; two million women were pulled into the workforce to take the places of male workers drafted to the battlefield (Marlow, 1998). On top of this, 100,000 women joined Britain's armed forces. The government provided nurseries in the most essential armaments factories to ensure women could get out to work; by 1917, more than 100 had opened across the country.[1] Nothing like this had ever been seen in Britain before.

The mass influx of women into factory work led to other changes. For example, women working with explosives couldn't wear any metal, so corsets were put aside; long hair got in the way on the production line, so many women went for easy-to-look-after bobs; long skirts were impractical, so trousers and even shorts became common. The women who came out of the war not only looked very different to the Edwardian women of the prewar years but were also different in more profound ways. They had undertaken jobs that people, including many women, had previously thought were only suitable for men. They had experienced financial and personal freedom that they could only have imagined before the war, when 1.7 million women had been trapped in domestic service – a peak never matched again. Ethel Dean was one such woman. She worked at the munitions factory at Woolwich Arsenal in London, and said: 'When you were in service you couldn't go out when you liked. When you work in the factories you've got your own time, haven't you? You just go home of a night, wherever you live, and you can go out when you like'. Women workers did face discrimination at work – many were paid lower rates than men. In some cases, they fought for equality despite the pressure to keep the war effort going. For example, in one dispute over the size of a war bonus paid out in 1918, women workers led and won a strike on the buses and trams in London for equal pay with men. Such experiences led historian Barbara Drake to write in 1920 that women had learned valuable lessons during the war, most importantly: 'the power of organisation … and the value of their labour' (Drake, 1984, p108).

At the end of the war, many women found themselves pushed out of jobs as swiftly as they had been employed in them to make way for men returning from the war. Many expressed their unhappiness about losing the chance to earn a wage and live independently. But women's lives never entirely went back to prewar conditions. The vote was partly extended at the end of the war in 1918 to a minority of women with property or a university degree who were over 30, as well as to all men over

21, for the first time (Rowbotham, 1999). Working-class women were denied the vote for another decade – all women over 21 finally won the right to vote only in 1928. The politicisation of women workers and their experience of the war years spilled into the battles for access to birth control in the interwar years. Working-class women brought the questions of birth control, childcare and women's rights into the workplace and the unions. These could not be 'personal' issues for them; they couldn't be solved by individually adopting a different lifestyle, hiring nannies or paying for less dangerous illegal abortions. Working-class women's organisations became the driver for change over these issues because collective struggle was the only way the majority of women could achieve real change.

At an annual conference of Labour women in 1924, 200 delegates formed the Workers' Birth Control Group. They stated: 'We have now formed our Workers' Birth Control Group to make clear that we were working in and with the Labour Party and do not share the views of the extreme Malthusians, or the Eugenicists' notion that the poor were inferior stock'. (Hoggart, 1996, in Digby & Stewart, 1998, p145). The year after the 1926 general strike, Mrs Lawther (there is no record of her first name, which itself is a sign of times), a miner's wife from Durham, spoke at the Labour Party conference calling for birth control to be provided by local councils (Rowbotham, 1977a). She said that women deserved the backing of the miners and other trade unions because of the support they had given for the strike, and argued: 'It is four times more dangerous to bear a child as to work in a coalmine' (Rowbotham, 1977, p43).

In the 1920s, some volunteer-run birth control clinics were set up. Marie Stopes opened her first clinic in London in 1921, and also took a horse and adapted caravan out to provide a mobile clinic. Stella Browne regularly went around the country speaking to women's guilds, local Labour parties and co-ops on abortion and birth control, coining them 'theory and practice' talks (Brooke, 2013, p49). The Workers' Birth Control Group fought a long campaign to commit the Labour Party to support the provision of birth control advice at local authority clinics. This wasn't acted on until 1930, when for the first time local authorities had the right to give birth control advice. Much of the debate in the campaign was dominated by women's medical needs, their safety and better conditions for childbirth and maternity welfare. But the reason it took such a fight was because what lay beneath the arguments were questions of sexuality, autonomy and women's role as mothers. For example, campaigners were often at pains to point out they all had children, so as not to appear too radical or advocates of free love and promiscuity.

Another important victory for birth control campaigners was won when the Woman's Cooperative Guild voted in 1934 for reform of the abortion law, arguing:

> In view of the persistently high maternal death rate and the evils arising from the illegal practice of abortion, this Congress calls upon the government to revise the abortion laws of 1861 by bringing them into harmony with modern conditions and ideas, thereby making abortion a legal operation that can be carried out under the same conditions as any other surgical operation. (Francombe, 1984, p67)

Although the need for safe and legal abortion was posed as an alternative to the increased risks of the backstreet, the question of women's rights and freedom was part of the debate (Gaffin and Thomas, 1983, p107).

The Abortion Law Reform Association (ALRA) was launched in 1936 by women who had been active on the issue for some time, including Stella Browne, Janet Chance and Alice Jenkins (Francombe, 1984; Lewis 1984). Many were rooted in the labour movement's 'latticework of socialist, feminist and working women's organisations' (Brooke, 2013, p101). ALRA also brought together doctors, lawyers and social campaigners who believed it was time the law was changed. It was to lead the lobbying for law reform for the next 30 years. ALRA did try to attract working-class activists into its ranks and promoted a penny membership; 734 such members had joined by 1939. It gave out leaflets asking: 'Do you want the abortion laws changed?' directed aimed at working women and men (Brooke, 2013, p101). Several working-class women spoke out at ALRA's founding conference. One was a nurse who had won local support when she was sacked from her job as a health visitor in Edmonton for giving advice on birth control back in 1922. She made it clear that she saw abortion as a class issue, saying: 'Poor women live under the spell of fear and they are always trying to get themselves right. Working women want abortion. Why should not the poor have it? Let the poor have what the rich have already got' (in Widgery, 1975).

In 1937, under pressure to address the question of abortion, the government set up the Interdepartmental Committee on Abortion to look into 'the prevalence of abortion, and the present law relating thereto, and to consider what steps can be taken by more effective enforcement of the law or otherwise to secure the reduction of maternal mortality and morbidity arising from this cause' (Brookes, 2013, p105). It published a report in 1939, which showed just how widespread backstreet abortions were: 'between 110,000 and 150,000 abortions were carried out annually, and of these 40% were criminally induced'. The questions from Norman Birkett, Chair of the Committee, during the inquiry reveal as much about contemporary views as the report itself. At one point, he questions ALRA Chair Janet Chance, asking: 'Have you considered how frequently a 14th or 15th child in a family has become a very great man?' She replied: 'have you considered how rapidly maternal death rises after the fifth child?' (In Potts et al., 1977, p287). Dorothy Thurtle, the only working-class woman on the panel, was Labour Leader of Shoreditch Council and daughter of Labour MP George Lansbury. She produced what fellow ALRA member Janet Chance called a courageous minority report about the reality of working-class women's experiences and their need for change (Hindell and Simms, 1971). Dorothy Thurtle became Vice Chair of ALRA after the Second World War.

Once again, the outbreak of war curtailed the campaign. The Second World War meant that the question of abortion law was put aside, but actual abortion numbers increased. Women again poured into what had been male-only jobs in numbers that surpassed the peaks reached during the First World War. As many as 75% of new workers were married women; up to 3 million married women and widows eventually joined the workforce representing double the prewar figures. Over 100,000 women also joined various branches of the armed forces, and more than 80,000 made up the Land Army billeted to work on farms across the country.[2] This opened up a whole new world for millions of women. In order to ensure the munitions factories were working at full capacity, the government set up crèches, some of them open 24 hours for round-the-clock shifts. 2,000 'British restaurants' were also opened so that workers could eat cheaply, and shoppers were even provided who would queue for rationed food for women in the arms factories (Longmate, 2002). The numbers of school children receiving free milk and school dinners also rose. Suddenly the state was finding the resources to help carry some of the burden of women's role in the family because it needed women's labour to win the war. Women worked long hours in heavy, dirty and sometimes dangerous jobs, but they also earned money and enjoyed unprecedented personal and sexual freedom. For the many without reliable and affordable contraception, this led to high numbers of unwanted pregnancies. The number of married women having abortions doubled during the war, and the number of 'illegitimate' births soared to one third of all births by 1945 (Humphries and Gordon, 1994).

When the war was over, the nurseries closed and the support the government had been so keen to offer working women to lighten the burden of domestic labour was wound down. Many women were laid off to allow returning soldiers back into employment. They were encouraged to see the family and domestic sphere as the centre of their life and responsibility. But once again it was impossible for women's lives to be pushed back in time completely (Roberts, 1995). Their world was never going to be the same. The postwar boom meant that many women were quickly pulled into new industries and the expanding education system. These developments exposed a growing gap between how women were treated and their dramatically changing expectations, which opened up new struggles that were to transform the political landscape of the 20th century.

The experiences of women several millennia ago, through to the early campaigners and those who documented the lived experiences of working-class women, are still valid to this very day. They taught us that women cannot play a full role in society while they can't control their fertility. They also showed that, whatever the law and state of medical knowledge, working-class women have consistently been denied the best available birth control and abortion services that wealthy women have always been able to access. By the 1960s, the pressure to change the law became inescapable.

FOUR

An Act of liberation?

The Abortion Act 1967 made it possible for hundreds of thousands of women to access legal, safe and free abortions in Britain for the first time. Veteran campaigner for women's reproductive rights, Dr Wendy Savage, has said of the impact of the Act that it 'virtually eliminated deaths from unsafe abortions in Great Britain and freed women from the nightmare of unplanned pregnancy'.[1] It was the culmination of years of campaigning and pressure from below from women, the labour movement, medical staff and ALRA. Liberal MP David Steel led the Bill, but a sympathetic Labour government helped enable its success. The passing of the Bill was a sign of changing times. Over the same period of a few years the death penalty was abolished, homosexuality decriminalised for those over 21, divorce made easier and free contraception made more widely available regardless of age and marital status. The Equal Pay Act 1970 followed the magnificent strike by women at Ford Dagenham, which put the issue in the spotlight, and in 1975 the Sex Discrimination Act was passed. The BBC heralded the developments with the headline 'New laws to end battle of the sexes'.[2]

The 1960s saw a world ablaze with resistance and revolt. National liberation movements rose up in the colonies of empires old and new. France saw the biggest ever mass general strike in 1968. The Civil Rights Movement defied the racism of the US state. Mass struggles defined the era, and everything seemed possible. But society did not change overnight, and the position of women was full of contradictions – contradictions that would explode in their own movement very soon. In Britain in the early 1960's, the debate about abortion and changing the law reflected the fact that the past was refusing to disappear completely. The paternalism and class prejudice of the political and medical elites was stamped on the debates about abortion law and the eventual legislation (Hindell and Simms, 1971). The medical profession wanted to maintain control and avoid giving women complete autonomy, and many politicians wanted to limit legal abortion to those women they saw as 'deserving'. Law historian Sally Sheldon argues that this was about the state taking control of a situation to make abortion a medical issue, not a social one. She writes that women were 'decriminalised in order to be pathologised' (Sheldon, 1997, p21, p33). Legislating to allow 'abortion on demand' was portrayed as a great danger. Both sides used the phrase to illustrate a situation that had to be avoided to protect the morals and stability of society.

Although half a century old, and despite repeated challenges from anti-abortion campaigners, the Act has held up. Opponents have actively challenged it from its very inception and continue to attack its implementation to this very day. It is important to remember what the Act actually did and didn't do. It did not introduce abortion on demand. It did not stop abortion being treated as a criminal act. It simply, and importantly, created exclusions to the 1861 Act that allowed doctors to perform legal abortions and women to procure them if they fulfilled certain conditions (see Chapter Two). The law was not based on liberating women, though it contributed to women living more liberated lives. Instead, it focused on preventing the prosecution of doctors, stopping deaths from backstreet abortions and relieving the burden of women having too many children. Women's traditional role as mother and homemaker was not challenged. Many reformers continued to argue that access to legal abortion would enable women to better fulfil this 'natural' maternal role. Of course, and as has been pointed out, the glaring gap in its remit was and still is the fact that it was not extended to Northern Ireland, which at the time had its own government in Stormont.

Facts and fiction

A woman with an unwanted pregnancy in 1966 had limited options. But class prevailed over even these. If you had money, you could go to a private doctor, who might then send you to a private psychiatrist to sign you off as needing an abortion under the conditions established by Bourne in 1938 (see Chapter Two). One of ALRA's founders, Alice Jenkins, authored a 1960 book called *Law for the Rich*, which exposed how illegality disproportionally affected poor and working-class women. David Steel once remarked that Jenkins' book should have been called *Law for the Rich and Articulate*, because he became aware that such women could work the system and pay what was demanded (Steel, 2002). Journalist Paul Ferris wrote an influential book before the 1967 Act on the reality of abortion at the time. He said he found that the women who could most easily access legal abortions 'were the sort of people who belong to consumer organisations, know their MP, and send the wine back' (Ferris, 1966, p33). There were an estimated 10,000 such private abortions carried out annually until the new law was enacted in 1968.

But even as the law stood still in the years leading up to 1967, facts on the ground were changing fast. An increasing number of abortions were taking place in NHS hospitals: from 2,300 in 1961 to 9,700 by 1967 (Ferris, 1966, p137). This was a sign that doctors were using the widest understanding of the Bourne judgement to treat women and save lives. But if you didn't have money and couldn't persuade a doctor that you deserved an NHS abortion, there was no other alternative but some form of the backstreet (Rowe, 1984). In many cases, this may have been self-medicating with a syringe and soap, or getting 'something from the pharmacy' in a practice that reached back through generations.

It is impossible to accurately state the number of backstreet abortions that took place in the early 1960s, but it is estimated that it was up to 100,000 (Sheldon, 1997). Illegality meant the procedure was cloaked in secrecy. Many women attempted abortion themselves but failed; midwives reported women showing concern for the condition of their newborn baby because of what they had ingested during the pregnancy. Calculations of the number of women who died every year from unsafe abortions are also hard to pin down, as even doctors who knew the real cause of death may have refrained from recording it (Ferris, 1966). Figures from before the introduction of antibiotics indicate that at least 500 women died every year between 1926 and 1937 (Hindell and Simms, 1971). In response to a question from pro-reform MP Renee Short in 1965, Norman Pentland – Parliamentary Secretary, Ministry of Pensions and National Insurance – stated that 'between 250,000 and 350,000 working days were lost by working women each year due to abortion' (Hindell and Simms, 1971, p33). Home Office statistics stated that '30 to 50 women were dying as a result' of illegal abortions every year (Dyhouse, 2013, p168). By 1966, illegal abortion was the 'chief cause of avoidable maternal death' (Brookes, 2013, p133). Consultant obstetrician and gynaecologist Kathleen Firth described her experiences when abortion was still illegal:

> Before 1967 if one visited a postmortem room there were always two particular dead bodies there. One was the lilac coloured person, accidently or purposely dead through coal gas poisoning. The other was the young thing discovered in her bathroom with a Higginson Syringe and a bowl of soapy water, dead from soap or air embolism … A pupil nurse was discovered in the corridor of the Nurses' Home, collapsed and bleeding with her blood only 30% of the normal density. In her room was discovered a curved knitting needle which had been sheathed with rubber tubing. (NAC, 1992)

In Scotland, where abortion was still governed by common law, one doctor in Aberdeen, Sir Dugald Baird, pioneered a comprehensive service for women. He showed what was possible. Between 1937 and when he retired in 1965, his hospital staff provided birth control and abortions within the NHS, giving women the greatest reproductive choices of any part of the UK at the time (Hindell and Simms, 1971).

The fate of women forced to take the biggest risks and the reality of dangerous abortion practices and prosecution were increasingly portrayed in the media in the early 1960s. Newspaper reports told of the horrific experiences of women's backstreet abortions, including describing the plight of women who had been blinded after taking doses of quinine to terminate an unwanted pregnancy (Hindell & Simms, 1971). When Paul Ferris published his book on abortion in 1966, he described the letters he received from women desperate for help after he wrote two articles about it in *The Observer* newspaper (Ferris, 1966). Such was the sense of taboo and secrecy surrounding abortion that anyone who went public was a beacon for women looking for a way out of their predicament. ALRA itself received letters from women asking for abortions; its administrator, Dilys Cossey, described women arriving at the door of her flat (which was listed as the office address for some years) begging for help to get an abortion.[3]

Abortion has always been an everyday fact of life, but public references had been as oblique and hidden even in fiction as they had to be in real life. Abortions have long been referred to in novels, plays and poetry through the years of illegality and beyond. Archivist Lesley Hall has gathered a fascinating list of references to abortion both 'achieved' and 'contemplated' on her Literary Abortion webpage.[4] But in the early 1960s, the hidden reality was finally coming out in to the open. In the days of few television channels, a reference to abortion on television had a huge impact. Many who campaigned for legal abortion refer to an episode of the popular TV BBC soap of the time, *Doctor Finlay's Casebook*, which was broadcast in July 1965 and featured an abortion. Leading ALRA member Diane Munday still recalls the impact of its screening on highlighting the need for a change in the law (Munday, 2017, interview with author).

Films and plays that featured abortion faced heavy censorship. For example, the British Board of Film Censors (BBFC) demanded many changes after reading the film script based on Alan Sillitoe's novel *Saturday Night and Sunday Morning* before its release in 1960. One BBFC reader, giving an opinion on what certificate the film should be allocated, commented: 'I think most of what happens is tolerable for "X", but I have strong misgivings about the slaphappy and successful termination of pregnancy, which seems to be very dangerous stuff for our younger X cert customers' (Aldgate, 1995, p91). The script was adapted, and the abortion was rewritten to appear to be unsuccessful. The censor wrote: 'I am very glad this change has been made'. An abortion scene in the 1963 theatre production of *Alfie* was heavily vetted by the Lord Chamberlain's office, which controlled theatre censorship at the time. Among the many changes demanded was the toning down of a scene showing an abortion. When it came to the film version of *Alfie*, released in 1966, the BBFC commented: 'These are strong scenes, but they will probably be acceptable in the context, since they do make a valid point against abortion. We would not want any really harrowing moans and screams' (Aldgate, 1995, p113).

These interventions make director Ken Loach's hard hitting adaptation of the novel *Up the Junction* for the BBC's Wednesday Play slot in 1965 all the more remarkable. Unusually, Loach combined facts and the voice of a real doctor calling for a change in abortion law with the fictional story of young women, their relationships and what happened to one who had to go through a backstreet abortion.[5] Cossey remembers Loach calling to collect ALRA briefing material to ensure his portrayal was accurate. The Wednesday Plays aimed to address the most contested social issues of the day, including racism, homosexuality and the death penalty. *Up the Junction* was broadcast as Steel's Bill was being debated, and was intended to intervene in the debate. The BBC received a record 400 complaints about the play and its portrayal of young people's sex lives, but the play reached an audience of 10 million people. This is the equivalent of popular soaps and shows such as *Strictly Come Dancing* today, and it made a profound impact.

Abortion was not just being addressed on television. Popular 'agony aunt' of the time, Marje Proops, wrote in the *Daily Mirror* in 1964 that the abortion laws 'favour the well-heeled' (Brooke, 2013, p158). This was when the *Daily Mirror* was Britain's bestselling newspaper with a circulation of 5 million.[6] During the same period, Oxford students organised a 1,000-name petition to the Prime Minister calling for a change in the law after a woman student died after an abortion (Hindell and

Simms, 1971, p123). The situation for women facing unwanted pregnancies could no longer be covered up.

The 1960s campaign

As the previous chapter described, many of the founders of ALRA had been active in the Labour Party and wider labour movement. In the 1950s, its AGMs included many delegates from Women's Cooperative Guilds and Labour women's sections. But its middle-class leadership came to concentrate on proving themselves respectable in order to lobby and win the political and medical establishments over to its views (Brooke, 2013). The 1960s saw a new young generation, including Diane Munday and Madeleine Simms, join and completely reinvigorate the campaign. Vera Houghton, who had been a member since the 1950s, was Chair and seen as the indispensable hub of the campaign. Although the organisation was changing with the times, some past conventions still endured. Cossey remembers that throughout the campaign they all addressed each other formally as 'Mrs Munday' and so on.[7] She recalled the times, saying: 'So it was as though the lid was coming off a number of issues that had been repressed. Women were becoming more articulate. Women of our generation – like Diane and Madeleine – realised that this was a long overdue reform' (Cossey, 2002). Diane Munday broke ground by being open in meetings and on the radio about having had an abortion. She faced hostility from taking a public stand, which included her local grocery shop refusing to serve her.

ALRA was never a mass organisation – the membership stood at 1,120 in 1966. But it established a high profile and targeted MPs relentlessly with information about the reality of illegal abortions and shifting public opinion. It spent a lot of resources on polling; one poll it commissioned in 1966 indicated that as many as 600,000 women may have undergone illegal abortions since 1946 (Brooke, 2013). ALRA contacted parliamentary candidates even before they were elected to build a side in parliament for a change in the law. David Steel first came into contact with ALRA during the 1966 General Election, when he answered their enquiry about his views by saying he would support abortion law reform (Steel, 2002). Later in the year, when his name came up third in the Private Member's Bill ballot, ALRA immediately approached him to take up the baton for abortion law reform and he read Alice Jenkins' book. He almost didn't select abortion law for his Bill, intending to pursue a Bill on another central social issue: the decriminalisation of homosexuality. But he was persuaded of the need to champion a Bill on abortion and picked up the substance of a previous Bill by Lord Silkin. By this time there had already been a number of failed attempts to change the law on abortion, and there was no reason to think this time would be different (Potts et al, 1977). But by the mid-1960s the desire for change could not be ignored, as women with different expectations of their lives came crashing against social mores and legal constraints they were no longer willing to endure.

The impact of the thalidomide scandal became a factor in the debates. Thalidomide was a drug prescribed as a mild sedative for morning sickness and sleeplessness in the late 1950s and early 1960s. But it was discovered that thousands of women worldwide who had taken it had miscarriages, stillbirths and gave birth to severely disabled babies, many of whom did not survive. Women who discovered they had taken the drug were denied the right to have an abortion. Another factor was the role the Labour government played in facilitating the Bill. Steel and other campaigners cite the importance of support from key Labour cabinet ministers who wanted to see a change in the law and ensured the Bill was given vital extra time on two occasions:

> Roy Jenkins was Home Secretary, Dick Taverne was his junior minister, who was the one who came to pursue me immediately, the day the ballot was announced … Kenneth Robinson was Minister of Health and he was the author of one of the six previous attempts to legislate. Because there had been six bills between 1953 and 1967, none of which had found parliamentary time, but Kenneth Robinson's was one of them. So you had the Minister of Health, who was openly committed to this cause, you had as the government Chief Whip John Silkin, whose

> father had been the promoter of the Bill in the Lords, which I had inherited, and you had Douglas Houghton as chairman of the Parliamentary Labour Party, whose wife was the chairman of ALRA. (Steel, 2002)

What were the key arguments?

First, even for most of the proponents for change, reform was not about giving women free access to abortion. Women were not going to be allowed to decide whether or not they wanted to carry a pregnancy to full term. It was to be treated as a medical question, and doctors were to be given ultimate control in deciding whether a woman could be allowed an abortion. So, the debates were dominated by discussion about what factors doctors could take into account when deciding. For example, in November 1966, the BMA and the Royal College of Obstetricians and Gynaecologists (RCOG) published a report rejecting any so-called 'social clause' and ruling out a clause allowing abortion in the case of rape or sex under the legal age of 16 (Brooke, 2013). Doctors were concerned that women might assume they would *automatically* be allowed an abortion if they had been raped, as if this was somehow an objectionable expectation. Such a clause was seen as an unacceptable drift towards abortion on demand, and doctors lobbied for specific mention of rape, incest and pregnant underage girls to be left out of the Bill (Hindell and Simms, 1971). Instead, they insisted, they should be 'trusted' to take into account such matters when a woman came to them requesting an abortion.

The medical establishment wanted to keep the conditions under which abortion was allowed to strictly measurable medical conditions. There was sharp debate about including any 'social clause', which would allow a woman's social and economic conditions as well as medical needs to be considered. Early drafts of the Bill included such a social clause, which stated that an abortion should be allowed if 'the pregnant woman's capacity as a mother will be severely overstrained by the care of a child or of another child'. One campaigning doctor in the World League for Sexual Reform mocked the double standards of a society in which having money meant you could access an abortion but lack of it meant you were denied one: 'When doctors maintain that they will have nothing to do with termination of pregnancy on social grounds this must be taken to mean poverty is not regarded as an adequate indication while wealth on the other hand is' (Widgery, 1975, p4).

Steel amended his original draft under pressure and eventually took out a separate 'social' clause. Instead, the phrase 'the patient's total environment actual or reasonably foreseeable' was inserted as something to be considered by doctors. ALRA was very unhappy about this and other compromises made as the Bill proceeded through parliament. These included the requirement for two doctors to agree an abortion and the right of doctors to refuse to do them. But in the end, the majority felt that Steel's Bill looked like the best chance of change, so continued their support despite their concerns (Brooke, 2002). Steel defends his changes, saying he felt he was successful in bundling the social clause into what a doctor could consider and so making it harder for the clause to be dropped in amendments. ALRA activists knew that each line of any new law would have a direct impact on hundreds of thousands of people's lives, so they fought hard for every word. They camped out in the Houses of Parliament, talking to MPs at every opportunity (Hindell and Simms, 1971). Campaigners remember that at the time parliament was quite open, and it was easy to wander around and accost MPs at any time of the day or night. Diane Munday used to simply pull her car up, park at St Stephen's entrance to the House of Commons and walk in.

Moral judgements about women were woven through every debate. Anti-reform MPs even claimed that women would suddenly want abortions if they were legal, as if they were a new brand of confectionery. Labour MP Anne Kerr asked: 'Would my hon. Friend not agree that the Bill, if carried, will give the green light to many girls and women who would not otherwise want to have abortions? That is what worries me'.[8] Such patronising views ignored the fact that women who want abortions have always existed, so much so that illegality and health risks had not deterred them. Rank hypocrisy was often on display. One MP, Peter Mahon, argued that legal abortion should not be allowed because; 'Let me remind Parliament, if with the smug complacency of Englishmen it is anxious to forget, that we have had a Prime Minister and a Foreign Secretary who were the illegitimate children of servant girls'.[9] Clearly it was not seen as smug complacency to ignore the life choices of 'servant girls' living in a society that deemed their offspring 'illegitimate' if they had not obtained a marriage certificate.

The wider social impact of the Bill's progress through its stages in Westminster was immense. During 1966 and 1967, 'throughout the country, political, religious, medical, women's and students' organisations all seemed to be discussing abortion law reform and passing resolutions recording their opinions' (Hindell and Simms, 1971, p187). Here was an issue that was not only illegal but had also been surrounded in stigma for generations – yet it was now being openly debated everywhere. Polls commissioned by ALRA and published during the Bill's process through parliament showed the public was in favour of a 'social' clause (Hindell and Simms, 1971). If the fusty MPs didn't see it, then the general public did – abortion was a social issue; a class issue. It seemed logical to many that questions of poverty and other material matters had a real impact on why women might need an abortion. It seemed logical, then, that such factors should be taken into account.

ALRA was almost overwhelmed by requests to send speakers to meetings across the country. This included debates with newly established anti-abortion group the Society for the Protection of Unborn Children (SPUC), which was launched to organise opposition to the Bill[10] (Munday, 2017, interview with author). As momentum for reform grew, the anti-abortion lobby, which had been caught out by the level of support for change both in and outside parliament, pulled out all the stops. Doctors who were willing to do abortions were compared to state executioners, referring to the abolition of the death penalty the year before. In a speech to a nurses' conference in 1966, Professor JS Scott of Leeds Medical School remarked: 'If parliament is legalising social abortion my suggestion is that the unemployed hangmen be retrained for service as state abortionists. It is bound to be a job after their own hearts – it should be no job of the medical and nursing profession' (Hindell and Simms, 1971, p188). Another doctor declared in the *Daily Mirror*:'We aren't butchers:We won't do it' (Hindell and Simms, 1971, p188).

The debate culminated in a second all-night sitting on the Bill. Its opponents attempted to make up for their lack of numbers by endless filibustering and trying to force last-minute compromises. Diane Munday remembers ALRA ensuring there were enough MPs in the House at all times for any vote, while maintaining a rota to allow MPs to take a break for a few hours' sleep in a room they had organised nearby (Munday, 2017, interview with author). Finally, on the morning of Friday 14 July, after a nonstop session of 13 hours and 20 minutes of debates and votes on amendments, the third and decisive reading in the Commons was accomplished. The Bill was still to go to the Lords, but it was now clear that the law was going to be changed and that MPs recognised its historic significance. Despite their exhaustion, Steel and MPs on both sides of the debate marked it with a further two hours of 'final' speeches.

Reading the Hansard record, one of these final speeches stands out. It was made by Labour MP Christopher Price, who had acted as one of the whips for the reformers, and it was not without its contradictions. He began by actually placating opponents and playing down the impact the new Bill would have, saying: 'many hon. Members have predicted a sort of headlong, gathering rush to abortion on demand when the Bill is passed. I should like to predict that for several years it will make very little difference'. But the section that marked itself out from the hours of debate was the final one. Virtually alone in the male-dominated Commons, he located the momentous vote they were about to take in the wider struggle outside parliament for women's rights, and recognised that this was where the pressure for change was strongest:

> The Bill will pass into law because of the demands of public opinion.When I have mixed with people both inside and outside the House who want the Bill, it has often occurred to me that it is not about abortion at all; it is part of the process of the emancipation of women which has been going on gradually over a very long period.

> The public opinion behind the Bill is millions of women up and down the country who are saying 'We will no longer tolerate this system whereby men lay down, as though by right, the moral laws, particularly those relating to sexual behaviour, about how women should behave'.[11]

An amendment by the Lords in the closing stages of their debate was illustrative of how strong the myths about the dangers of abortion still were. It came out of a discussion about how to define the level of risk to a woman's health that would allow a doctor to offer a termination. It was finally proposed to include the phrase that abortion would be legal if the health risks of carrying on the pregnancy were 'greater than if the pregnancy were terminated'. Even in 1967, the risks of a properly conducted abortion were less than a full-term pregnancy, so this last-minute amendment was to allow a wide interpretation of the law and make it difficult to challenge a doctor's decision to carry out an abortion (Hindell and Simms, 1971, p201). The Bill was finally passed on 27 October 1967. The Home Office asked for six months to prepare for implementation and to inspect nursing homes, so women had to wait until April 1968 before accessing their full rights.

One leading doctor declared in the *British Medical Journal* that the RCOG, like many MPs, had not expected any great change in practice after the Act, but wrote: 'How wrong we were' (Hindell and Simms, 1971, p214). Within a year, the number of abortions carried out in the NHS had more than doubled from the 1967 figure to 22,000; in 1969, another 33,000 took place, and in 1970 the figure was almost 50,000. On top of these were abortions carried out privately over the same period, which amounted to 15,000 in the first year, then 20,000, and in 1970 more than 30,000 (Hindell and Simms, 1971, p214).

Exceptions to the expansion of NHS provision were noticeable in the first year. In some cities, powerful sections of the medical establishment used their influence to block or undermine implementation of the Act. For example, NHS hospitals in Liverpool, Sheffield and Birmingham all had low abortion figures initially, reflecting anti-abortion sentiment among leading consultants, although this began to even up after the first year. It was in response to such anomalies that the Birmingham Pregnancy Advisory Service (later BPAS) was first launched. In fact, because of the 'notorious hostility' of Birmingham gynaecologists to the Abortion Act, at first even BPAS abortions for Birmingham women were carried out in London (Hindell and Simms, 1971).

As the next chapter will show, the first attacks on the Bill from anti-abortion campaigners came within months of it becoming law. One amendment tried to insert a 'consultant clause', something that had been attempted during the readings of the original Bill. This would have limited the number of abortions allowed, as only consultants could agree them. Other opponents of the Bill claimed that private doctors were profiteering from providing abortion and that women from abroad were flowing in to take advantage of the law. Such opponents pushed for an enquiry into how the law was working, which the Tory government of 1970 instituted under Justice Lane in 1971. After sitting for three years, the committee reported in 1974 and came out in support of the Act, stating: 'we are unanimous in supporting the act and its provisions. We have no doubts that the gains facilitated have much outweighed any disadvantages for which it has been criticised'. It argued for expanding NHS services to reduce the use of the private sector, and recommended specifying a time limit of 24 weeks. The report also contained remarks aimed at the predicted response of anti-abortionists, who had been so keen to investigate the Act because they assumed the committee would be critical of it:

> Our generally tolerant attitude may disappoint those who see the act and its workings as evidence of a serious and progressive decline in the standards and in sexual behaviour in this society. We understand this point of view and we sympathise with the motives of those who, disturbed by contemporary evidence of licence, press for action to curtail it.

The one amendment to the Bill that succeeded was contained in the Human Fertilisation and Embryology Act 1990, which created the 24-week time limit. In fact, the 1967 Act did not contain any time limit; the 28-week limit that existed before 1990 was based on the Infant Preservation Act 1929, which stated: 'evidence that a woman had at any material time been pregnant for a period of twenty-eight weeks or more shall be prima facie proof that she was at that time pregnant of a child capable of being born alive'.[12] However, at the same time as bringing down the general abortion time limit, the 1990 changes liberalised aspects of the law by removing any time limit in the specific conditions referred to in Chapter Two.

The next chapter will show how the anti-abortion lobby took up the fight to push back the new freedoms opened up by the Act, and how it had to change tactics as the benefits of legal and safe abortion access became widely accepted. The dangers of the backstreet were still in many people's memories, and they did not want to go back to it. The emergence of the Women's Liberation Movement alongside an active Left and a period of militant working-class struggle ensured legal abortion was vigorously defended in the years that followed 1967.

FIVE

Opposition and resistance

The fights for abortion rights in the US and Britain take place in different contexts. This chapter, on the politics of the anti-abortion movement and the pro-choice response, will concentrate on Britain. But it will also include reference to the US because the anti-abortion movement there has undoubtedly had an influence on debates and actions in the UK. Every attack from the anti-abortionists in Britain has been met with resistance and a defence of legal and safe abortion. This chapter will look at how the struggle to defend legal abortion after 1967 mobilised new forces to defend a woman's right to access full reproductive health care including abortion. This pro-choice defence, most recently witnessed in the worldwide anti-Trump protests, has often forced the anti-abortion lobby to adopt new tactics; they have shown they will continue to fight on every front to deny women the right to choose.

Support for the new law in Britain quickly took root after April 1968, as hundreds of thousands of women saw they no longer had to risk their life to end an unwanted pregnancy. Support for legality has remained strong in Britain to this day. This has meant the dominant arguments from the anti-abortionists in Britain have been a constant drip feed of criticism and legal challenges based on the claim that getting abortions should be more controlled. Such anti-abortion campaigners say they do not oppose every abortion and that it can be allowed in very limited circumstances; for example, to save the life of a woman, or if a woman has been raped or is underage. Of course, outright opponents of abortions who argue that all abortion is murder regardless of the circumstances still exist. These declare that the embryo is another human being from the moment of conception. Although open proponents of a complete ban on all abortions are a minority in the British anti-abortion lobby, they are an increasingly vocal one (Hayes and Lowe, 2015).

Pickets

Abortion providers Marie Stopes and BPAS report a rise in aggressive pickets of abortion clinics in Britain in recent years. Anti-abortion organisations such as Abort67 and 40 Days for Life are at the forefront of these, as well as other religious groups such as Helpers of God's Precious Infants. Genevieve Edwards of Marie Stopes UK told *The Guardian* that clinics sometimes have to let women attending a clinic know in advance about the pickets: 'We do telephone women the day beforehand to warn them if there is a particularly large protest planned, so we can tell them the least obtrusive route into the clinic and offer to escort them inside' (Smith, 2015). Such tactics, and sometimes the groups themselves, are often imported from the US. For example, 40 Days for Life was founded in Texas in 2014. Its intimidating pickets outside abortion clinics in England, Wales and more recently Scotland last 40 days to mirror the Christian festival of Lent. 40 Days for Life expanded their targets in Scotland during a three-month international campaign in 2017 to include hospitals in Edinburgh, Aberdeen and Dundee.[1]

Sometimes pickets film women entering clinics and try and thrust models of foetuses into their hands or stand in front of them with huge blown-up 'photos' of foetuses. Pro-choice activists have stood in solidarity with women and staff attending clinics and sometimes successfully forced anti-abortion pickets to move away. For example the Abortion Rights group in Cardiff organises counter-protests against 40 Days for Life, who have picketed the BPAS clinic there since 2013. The anti-abortionists have been forced to move a distance from the clinic. In some cases, the persistence of picketing has led to calls for 'buffer zones' outside such clinics. Running the gauntlet of hostile protesters is often traumatic and intimidating for women and clinic staff. One study offered staff and women attending abortion clinics in England a comment form to record their reactions (Hayes and Lowe, 2015). The study concluded that even the presence of a picket caused distress. But in many cases women and staff reported feeling harassed by the actions of anti-abortion pickets. One woman reported:

> I was disgusted and annoyed to have been stopped while approaching the door of the building by an abortion protester. At a difficult enough time as it is, the last thing I and my partner needed was this kind of intervention, adding more stress to an already stressful situation. (p13)

Another described her feelings seeing protesters outside the clinic in Milton Keynes: 'when arriving people were outside with signs, it made me scared to come in and I was physically shaking' (p21). Another comment from a woman attending a clinic at Bedford Square in central London reported that she felt 'harassed and violated' when picketers filmed her without her consent (p24).

Mind your language

Language is very important to the anti-abortion lobby. They coined themselves 'pro-life', implying that pro-choice campaigners are pro-death. One anti-abortion organisation is simply called Life. These groups are careful always to refer to the 'unborn baby', even if it is a two-week embryo; the pregnant woman is always the 'mother'. Some even try to hijack the slogans of the pro-choice movement saying 'the baby has to have a choice' (Faludi, 1992, p443). Some anti-abortion campaigns in the US have even invented terms to describe abortions, including 'partial birth abortion', making the process as much a part of the argument as the end result (Grimes and Brandon, 2014). More recently they refer to 'dismemberment abortions', even though this too is not a medically recognised term or procedure. Using such language has only one purpose: to try make people recoil at the idea of abortion and build opposition to any terminations.

At the same time, increasingly progressive-sounding language is used to hide the real purpose of proposals around abortion access.

Insisting on statutory counselling or waiting times between asking for and accessing an abortion are posed as 'empowering' women. SPUC claims that true feminists are pro-life.[2] The cause of women's rights was also cited when Tory MP Fiona Bruce put an amendment to the 2015 Serious Crime Bill to prevent abortions for 'sex selection'. Bruce and anti-abortion campaigners claimed sex-selection abortions favouring males was a major issue in Britain, making a ban on them a women's rights question. Newspapers ran sensationalist headlines referring to the 'lost girls' that had been aborted.[3] But the figures they used didn't add up – there was simply no evidence for their claims. The Department of Health had published a report on sex ratios at birth in England and Wales in 2014, and concluded that 'no group is statistically different from the range that we would expect to see naturally occurring'.[4] Bruce's amendment was defeated after pro-choice campaigners fought a determined campaign to expose the real facts behind the claims and what the consequences would be of passing what they coined a 'Trojan Horse' amendment.[5] The proposal was an attempt to put a feminist gloss on a move that would have actually limited women's rights, and also had racist undertones (it attributed the blame for sex selection to ethnic minorities).

Conservative anti-abortion campaigner and head of the anti-choice Population Research Institute in the US, Steven Mosher, revealed the real agenda beneath such tactics. He laid out his strategy in 2008, which is worth quoting at length to expose its full cynicism:

> I propose that we – the pro-life movement – adopt as our next goal the banning of sex-selective abortion. By formally protecting all female foetuses from abortion on the ground of their sex, we would plant in the law the proposition that the developing child is a being whose claims on us should not depend on their sex.
>
> This sense of contradiction will be further heightened among radical feminists, the shock troops of the abortion movement. They may believe that the right to abortion is fundamental to women's

> emancipation, but many will recoil at the thought of aborting their unborn sisters. How can they, who so oppose patriarchy and discrimination on the basis of sex, consent to the ultimate form of patriarchy and discrimination, namely, the elimination of baby girls solely on account of their sex? Many, it is safe to predict, will be silent, while others will raise their voices, but with less conviction.
>
> While the pro-aborts are stammering and stuttering, we pro-lifers will be advancing new moral and logical arguments against the exercise of the 'right' to an abortion solely on the grounds of sex or race … In these and other ways, the debate over this legislation will not subtract from, but add to, the larger goal of reversing Roe v Wade and, ultimately, passing a Human Life Amendment.[6]

In a similar tack, anti-abortion campaigners say they are standing up for disability rights when they argue for a ban on all abortions carried out because of foetal abnormalities. We live in a society where disabled people routinely face discrimination in many areas of their lives and having an impairment can mean suffering exclusion and prejudice. Successive governments have scapegoated disabled people and cut vital benefits that make it possible for disabled people to live full and independent lives. As has been explored in previous chapters, state-sanctioned eugenicist policies have targeted people with impairments, among others (Tilley et al., 2012). Such experience of oppressive policies and injustice must be taken into account when concerns are raised about abortions for foetal abnormalities. But anti-abortion groups that oppose abortions on the basis of foetal abnormalities rarely have genuine concerns about the difficulties disabled people face; instead, they use the argument to cut back on women's rights to choose abortion.

Campaigns for women to have control over their reproductive choices need to be concerned about how disabled people are treated in society. Britain's national Abortion Rights campaign states that it 'fully supports the rights of disabled people and supports the work of the disability rights movement to change society for the fullest recognition of rights and participation of all people'.[7] The modern abortion rights movement also argues that being pro-choice means women who have in the past been denied the right to have children should have the right to have a family. This means disabled people (women and men) should have the right to have and raise children and receive any support that may be needed.

Banning abortions for foetal abnormalities does nothing to address the real issues disabled people experience; at the same time, it imposes an obligation on a woman to carry an unwanted pregnancy to term. Currently, abortions carried out for this reason are a tiny proportion of the total – 2%.[8] Supporting a woman's right to abortion if she decides she cannot carry a pregnancy to full term for any reason, including if she finds out that the foetus has a serious abnormality, does not equate to being anti-disabled people in society. A woman who opts for abortion when she finds her foetus is affected by an impairment is not advocating some eugenicist agenda, nor is she making a statement about people with that or any other impairment. The decision whether or not to have a baby is one that can only be made by the pregnant woman herself. Only she will know what she feels capable of giving to the upbringing of any child, based on her own experiences and material circumstances. She may already have children or she may already have a disabled child or feel she will not receive the support she would need. The decision must be hers and not the courts' or doctors'.

Abortion opponents paint scenarios in which the pregnant woman is portrayed as the enemy of the foetus she is carrying. She is demonised as selfish or prejudiced without anyone knowing the full extent of her situation and experiences. The only alternative offered to her is to be told she must carry her pregnancy to full term against her consent. This debate came to the fore in 2016, as new noninvasive tests for Down's syndrome became available. Some of the worries expressed about the tests represented genuine concerns that negative preconceptions about Down's syndrome and children born with the condition need to be challenged – and they do. But the anti-abortion lobby uses such concerns to make it acceptable to deny women access to information about their own bodies – for example, by restricting information from pregnancy scans – because it disapproves of how they may choose to act on it.

Informed choice

Anti-abortion campaigners have often used the question of what information or counselling women requesting an abortion should receive as a way to put more hurdles in women's way in the name of 'empowerment'. But calls for statutory 'counselling' insult women. A woman who comes to an abortion clinic having requested an abortion knows what she is doing; she has thought about it, and her autonomy should be respected. When anti-abortion campaigners talk about the need to give women more information, what they really mean is they want to persuade the woman not to have an abortion at all. One study in Britain found only 9% of women took up pre-termination counselling; it concluded that the majority of women had already made their decision, and that any move towards compulsory counselling would go against women's wishes (Baron et al., 2015). Women shouldn't have to justify their decision to have an abortion to multiple people. They usually simply want to have it carried out quickly and safely. Those women who want to discuss their options are already offered counselling.

In September 2011, Tory MP Nadine Dorries lost an attempt to block abortion providers such as BPAS and Marie Stopes in Britain from offering counselling.[9] She claimed that such organisations had an interest in promoting abortion because they received public money for carrying them out, even though both are nonprofitmaking charities. In fact, BPAS reports that 16% of the women who come to them go on to decide to continue the pregnancy and have a baby (Furedi, 2016). This shows that non-judgemental support is already available. What Dorries and other anti-abortion campaigners actually wanted was for groups opposed to abortion to receive state funding for counselling services. Such groups already run what they call 'crisis pregnancy centres'. Adverts for these centres often mimic those of genuine abortion care clinics, but they are dedicated to scaring women into rejecting abortion as an option. In the past, such adverts were to be found in London Tube stations or at bus stops. Today, anti-abortion groups use the internet to try to masquerade as genuine services for abortion provision, investing in adverts that are rated higher in Google search results than real abortion provision (Grimes and Brandon, 2014). Successive undercover investigations into these centres have revealed the lies and scaremongering such groups use to frighten women into avoiding abortion. One such report, which Education for Choice (a project within the sexual advice charity, Brook) compiled in 2014, showed that:

> Two centres falsely linked abortion to an increased risk of breast cancer saying 'the only other thing that has been reported with quite strong evidence is the increase in the possibility of breast cancer following termination of pregnancy'. Oxford Care Centre (Life, December 2013)
>
> Counsellors fabricated or misrepresented other potential physical complications of abortion, with some centres claiming that abortion causes infertility: 'There's more risk of infertility from termination than there is from giving birth ... some reports will say as low as one percent risk of infertility from termination and some will say as high as 25%'. Central London Women's Centre (Good Counsel Network, November 2013)
>
> Ten centres claimed abortion caused 'Post Abortion Syndrome' claiming, 'For a lot of girls it's a lot like PTSD [Post Traumatic Stress Disorder], it's called Post Abortion Syndrome and it can come in varying degrees'. Acorn Pregnancy Centre, Stockport (Care Confidential, October 2013) (Education for Choice, 2014)

But 'Post Abortion Syndrome' is a fabricated notion, a 'bogus medical disorder, which is unrecognised by any medical body' (Biggs et al., 2016). The anti-abortion lobby wants to insist that abortion is a major and traumatic event for women. Opponents of abortion refuse to acknowledge that the most common feeling women report after an abortion is relief.[10] The people making it harder are the anti-abortion campaigners themselves. That's why there was so much anger in March 2017 at the news that the Tory government had given £250,000 raised from taxes on tampons and sanitary pads to the anti-abortion organisation Life.[11] Life said it would fund a homeless shelter for pregnant women. Pro-choice campaigners argued that it was bad enough for necessary sanitary items to be taxed as 'luxury' products, but for money generated by this 'tampon tax' to be given to an organisation that declares it won't give up until 'abortion is a thing of the past' was a 'bloody outrage'.[12]

Politics trumps science

The use of new technology to view a developing embryo and foetus has become a vital tool for the anti-abortion lobby – and not just in pickets outside clinics, with their giant posters. For example, the anti-abortion camp calls for mandatory viewing of ultrasound images of their pregnancy for women requesting abortion, and supposedly '4D' videos of foetus are used to build opposition to abortion.[13] As political scientist Rosalind Pollack Petchesky has shown, the use of images and films of the developing embryo suspended in space means that the woman becomes invisible and she argues, 'we have to restore women to a central place in the pregnancy scene. To do this, we must create new images that recontextualise the fetus, that place it back into the uterus, and the uterus back into the woman's body, and her body back into its social space' (Petchesky, 1987, p287). In a speech to the Midwives Alliance of North America in New York in 1992, academic Barbara Katz Rothman described this process: 'And finally we are left with the image of the foetus as a free-floating being, alone, analogous to man in space with the umbilical cord tethering it to the placental ship, and the mother reduced to the empty space that surrounds it' (Katz, 1992). Sally Sheldon rightly argues that as the terrain of the debate moves away from the needs of any particular woman, the social circumstances of her life and pregnancy are subordinated to the needs of the embryo or foetus, as defined by science or medicine (Sheldon, 1997).

Spinning bigotry as science was the motive behind the making of the discredited 1984 anti-abortion film *The Silent Scream*, which was made in association with the anti-abortion National Right to Life Committee (Petchesky, 1987). The doctor in a white coat fronting the film claims that advances in ultrasound technology enabled him to broadcast a foetus emitting a 'silent scream' of pain when an abortion begins. Planned Parenthood set up a panel of medical experts, who analysed the film's claims and its very blurred ultrasound images and published a rebuttal, *The Facts Speak Louder than The Silent Scream*,[14] which exposed the film as unscientific anti-abortion propaganda. The question of whether a foetus suffers pain has been the subject of much investigation. But current evidence still rules out the ability of a foetus to feel pain at the 12-week time period the film was discussing. When the RCOG was asked to look at the issue, they said there was no evidence that a foetus had developed the ability to feel pain before 24 weeks.[15]

This tactic of portraying women as no more than incubators, the environment of the foetus, remains favoured by anti-abortionists today (Shrage, 2002). In February 2017, an Oklahoma state legislator put forward a Bill that would not allow a woman to have an abortion without the written consent of the 'father of the foetus', in which he argued that the women's body was simply the 'host' of the foetus.[16] Such views have also shaped debates about pregnant women's responsibility to care for their pregnancies. Every pregnant woman deserves to be fully informed and supported to be healthy during her pregnancy. But in some regions of the US during the 1980s, women were prosecuted and criminalised when found drinking alcohol or taking prescription drugs, for example, because of the impact they could have on their foetuses (Faludi, 1992). Such behaviour was referred to as a form of child abuse (Faludi, 1992). The same moral outrage is rarely directed at the very real material impact that poverty, bad housing and long working hours have on the maternal health of millions of women.

Medical advances in neonatal care in the last 50 years have accompanied the development of visual technology. Opponents of abortion have argued that these medical advances mean that time limits for abortion in Britain should be brought down from the current 24-week limit. Remember the vast majority (92%) of abortions in Britain take place at or under 13 weeks' gestation, and 80% at or under 10 weeks' (Harker, 2016). The proportions are similar in the US. The American National Centre for Disease Control and Prevention reported that the majority (65.8%) of abortions are performed under 8 weeks' gestation, and nearly all (91.4%) are performed by 13 weeks' gestation. Only 7.2% of abortions in the US are performed between 14 and 20 weeks' gestation, and only 1.3% at 21 weeks' gestation.[17] In Britain in 2016, all abortions over 24 weeks' represent 0.1% of all abortions in England and Wales.[18]

There are many reasons why a woman might need an abortion at over 20 weeks of pregnancy. She might have not realised she was pregnant because she was menopausal, or as a young person was scared to admit she was pregnant until she could no longer hide it. Sometimes, delay in access can push women to a later abortion than necessary; this is particularly true for women who have to travel, or those who have experienced changed circumstances. A woman with a much-wanted pregnancy may have only found out that her foetus had a severe foetal abnormality in scans at 12 and 20 weeks. These scans need time to be analysed, and the woman needs time to absorb the information and decide what to do in what is often a deeply distressing situation. This can mean several weeks have passed.

The reality is that the minority of women who access abortion at this later stage are usually experiencing some of the most difficult and complex situations. Yet anti-abortion campaigns relentlessly attack time limits as a way of cutting back on abortions, even if the impact would only be on a small number of women – indeed, on some of the most vulnerable women in the direst need of access to abortion services. Neither does this stop politicians constantly pushing an argument that time limits are too high. For example, Secretary of State for Health, Jeremy Hunt, has argued to cut the time limit in half to 12 weeks, and Prime Minister Theresa May has voted for a 20-week limit in the past.[19] However, there is no pressure from medical opinion to make any changes. The BMA opposes changes to the current time limit; likewise, when the government asked the Science and Technology Committee to look at the question of time limits in 2007, it concluded there was no change in viability statistics and that no change in the law was needed.

But even if viability is now judged at 24 weeks for the purposes of abortion law, survival for a premature baby born this early is far from guaranteed. Healthy survival is only even a possibility if the birth takes place in a well-equipped hospital with availability of advanced medical resources, technology and specialist staff, which is what every parent will rightly want for their baby. But this situation cannot be compared to that faced by the very few women who need to access an abortion at this stage. As *The Guardian* columnist Polly Toynbee has written: 'The date at which a foetus might be viable has nothing to do with a woman's right to choose. Some day an embryo might be reared in a test tube to full term, but that changes nothing for a woman's right not to be a mother'.[20] Arguments about viability and its impact on abortion law became central to the debate around a Private Member's Bill put by Tory MP David Alton in 1987; he wanted to cut the limit to 18 weeks (Grahame, 1989). His Bill was talked out and provoked massive protests to defend abortion access and time limits; but it opened the door to new arguments about scientific justification of time limits on legal abortions. Sally Sheldon (1997) points to the dangers that pro-choice campaigners can face if they rely on framing their arguments within the terms of medical science. The attraction is that such arguments are often perceived as 'objective' and part of an approach that cites incontrovertible facts rather than opinions (Sheldon, 1997). But abortion is not simply a medical or scientific issue; it is political and personal. Science does not confer bodily autonomy on women. The right to have access to abortion and birth control has had to be fought for and defended in wider society.

Most anti-abortion campaigners use time limits as part of a strategy to oppose all abortion regardless of questions of viability, which are simply a useful concept to justify their position. So, for example, the British anti-abortion group, Abort67 (there is an equivalent organisation in the US called Abort73) has launched an initiative to target pre-12-week abortions. It is promoting a campaign to encourage pregnant women to talk about their pregnancy in the first trimester. This group describes the Abortion Act as the law that 'took away the protection in law of all human beings prior to birth'; they say they want people to become aware of what pregnancy in the first trimester means.[21] But, as Ann Furedi points out, 'women do not seek abortion because they are ignorant that the foetus is a potential child they seek an abortion precisely because they know it' (Furedi, 2016, p38).

US experience

In the US, aggressive picketing of abortion clinics has not been limited to shouting at, filming and jostling women patients and staff. The National Abortion Federation calculates that there have been 11 murders and 26 attempted murders of staff and security at abortion clinics since 1977. Three people were killed in a Planned Parenthood clinic in Colorado Springs in November 2015. Clinics routinely employ high-level security. After abortion clinic doctor George Tiller was murdered in 2009 – his was one of only three clinics in the US to carry out abortions after 21 weeks – staff continued to work in the clinic, which had in the past been firebombed, but wore bulletproof vests. Dr Willie Parker, an abortion care provider who works in the American South, argues that people working in these services would be 'naïve' not to recognise the very real dangers (see interview with Dr Willie Parker). He has a high national profile for the work he does, but he refuses to let threats deter him:

> I believe there are two ways to approach life: you can spend your time avoiding death or you can spend your time living. I know what I live for and I'm aware that people are trying to harm me and that harm could be lethal. So I take commonsense measures and do what I can to keep myself safe. But I refuse to be cowered into not living by my deeper conviction and that is one of humanity and the equality of women. (Interview with Dr Willie Parker)

Pickets intimidate, threaten and carry out violence, and their challenges to the law affect the rights of tens of thousands of women. In the US, the Supreme Court made a decision in June 2016 that was a major victory for reproductive rights campaigners by squashing parts of a Texas Bill of 2011 that deemed hundreds of abortion clinics illegal.[22] The spurious conditions anti-abortion campaigners wanted the bill to impose have been coined Trap (Targeted Regulation of Abortion Providers) laws by pro-choice campaigners. They were designed not with patients' health and safety in mind but with shutting down abortion provision. The Supreme Court struck down as 'unconstitutional' requirements stating that an abortion clinic dealing in medical abortions up to 12 weeks 'meet the same hospital-like building standards as an ambulatory surgical center' and that required doctors performing abortions to have admitting privileges at a nearby hospital.[23] Many states still have restrictive laws based on such conditions – the Center for Reproductive Rights tracked as many as 300 new restrictive conditions that have become state law since 2011 (out of 2,100 attempts).[24] The Supreme Court decision means these can be challenged and new attempts blocked. However, with Trump in the White House such legal victories cannot be guaranteed in the future.

The anti-abortion lobby's tactic of disguising bigotry in progressive clothing has also been displayed in the US through campaigns that equate Black women having abortions with committing racial genocide. One US anti-abortion group based in Texas, Life Always, paid for giant billboards featuring an African American child declaring: 'The most dangerous place for African Americans is in the womb'.[25] After protests, one four-storey-high billboard in Manhattan had to be taken down.[26] Other billboards used pictures of President Barack Obama with the caption: 'Every 21 minutes, our next possible leader is aborted'. In Georgia, one group ran billboards with a photo of a Black child, saying 'Black children are an endangered species' and advertising a website called 'toomanyaborted'.[27] Pro-choice and anti-racist campaigners voiced outrage at the campaign. Professor Beverly Guy-Sheftall, who teaches women's history and feminist thought at Spelman College, one of the US's oldest historically

Black colleges, said: 'To use racist arguments to try to bait black people to get them to be anti-abortion is just disgusting'.[28]

An Act to ban abortions based on race or sex, the Prenatal Nondiscrimination Act (Prenda), failed when it came to the House of Representatives in 2011. Yet for all the rhetoric about standing up for women, disabled people and Black people, every one of these campaigns would result in curbing rights, not extending them. This was recognised by a broad coalition of 24 organisations, which made a written statement to the House of Representative hearings on the Prenda Bill exposing the hypocrisy of those trying to push it through:

> We write to you as organizations concerned with protecting the rights and ensuring the wellbeing of women of color ... we refuse to allow race and gender to be wielded as a weapon to undermine abortion rights by decision makers who have never been friends to our community. For example, this year, Congress members Chabot (R-OH), Franks (R-AZ), Pence (R-Ind.), and Smith (R-TX) voted to defund family planning, ban abortion coverage in state health insurance exchanges, and allow providers to refuse abortion care even when a woman's life is in danger.[29]

The legislation is still being pursued through other avenues, and 38 states maintain Prenda legislation – including Arizona, which is the only state that prohibits abortions for reasons of race (If/When/How, 2016).

State laws have also led to US abortion providers in some states being required to inform prospective patients that, for example, having an abortion can cause breast cancer. This is despite there being absolutely no evidence to back up such a frightening claim. State-funded materials also repeat false assertions about negative health impacts of abortion:

> The Texas counseling booklet for patients states that complications of abortion 'may make it difficult or impossible to become pregnant in the future or carry

> a pregnancy to term'. State-produced materials that must be offered to patients in South Dakota state that infertility is a risk of abortion, without any qualification. (Vandewalker, 2012, p14)

One study found that: 'Eighty percent of crisis pregnancy centres listed in state resource directories for pregnant women provide misleading or false information regarding abortion' (Bryant et al., 2014, p601). The ethical problem of doctors giving unbalanced – or in some cases, plainly false – information is dismissed by those pushing for such misinformation to become mandatory: 'Abortion opponents have attempted to co-opt the doctrine of informed consent to further their political goal of reducing the number of abortions' (Vandewalker, 2012, p3).

The fight for access

One important difference between the abortion wars in Britain and the US is the battleground of funding. In Britain, the NHS provides free health care at the point of access and funds 98% of abortions (Harker, 2016). In contrast, in the US most individuals must pay for and organise private health-care insurance, sometimes as part of their job pay package. This means that anti-abortion campaigners can use challenges to funding rather than the actual procedure of abortion to block and undermine provision – with devastating effect. And this is why Trump's attacks on Planned Parenthood's funding are so dangerous.

When Barack Obama brought in the new health-care plan, the Affordable Care Act, one of the most rancorous debates was over the question of reproductive and abortion care. Under the Act, individual states can block or restrict insurance coverage of abortion; 25 states currently do this (Donovan, 2017). Insurance companies themselves can choose what they cover, and can refuse to cover contraception and abortion care. In one state. employees were told their health insurance would not cover contraception unless it was prescribed for an underlying health disorder, even though proving that would involve a gross invasion of a woman's privacy.

Restrictions on insurance cover started with the Hyde Amendment introduced in 1976. Marxist feminist Hester Eisenstein (2009) has written about the arguments that opposition to the Hyde Amendment raised within the pro-choice movement. The amendment did not affect legality, but its focus on funding disproportionally affected poor and Black women, who felt that better-off white women did not appreciate its impact. Under the Hyde Amendment, which Trump wants to make permanent, around 7.5 million low-income women were prevented from using their Medicaid coverage to obtain an abortion, except in the most extreme circumstances.[30] New research shows the extent to which restrictions on insurance coverage of abortion are affecting poorer and minority ethnic women (Donovan, 2017). Donovan (2017) points to the many different groups of women affected by insurance restrictions:

- Women enrolled in federal insurance programmes, including low-income women enrolled in Medicaid and the Children's Health Insurance Program and women with disabilities enrolled in Medicare;
- Federal employees, including civilian employees and their dependents, … military personnel and their dependents … and veterans who receive care through the Department of Veterans Affairs;
- Women who receive health care or coverage through federal programmes, including American Indians and Alaska Natives served by the Indian Health Service, women in federal correctional and immigration detention facilities, and Peace Corps volunteers.

Despite these attacks on funding, access and clinics, the pro-choice side in the US is defiant. The heroic work done by health-care staff and pro-choice activists in states intent on banning abortion provision by any means is a lifeline to millions of women. The banners that hang across the few remaining clinics in states such as Alabama, Mississippi and Texas declare: 'We stay open'. They show that the fight for reproductive rights in the US is far from over.

The defence of reproductive rights

Activists in the pro-choice movement in Britain today are the inheritors of decades of struggle for women's rights to control their bodies – both before and after the passing of the 1967 Act. The organisation Abortion Rights came out of the merger of ALRA, central to winning legal abortion in 1967, and the National Abortion Campaign (NAC), which successfully mobilised against subsequent attacks on the Bill from its formation in 1975. The political background of the development of the pro-choice side in Britain has some differences from the US experience. The trade union movement in Britain had a far greater density and social weight in the working class in the 1960s and 1970s, and there was also the strong presence of a social-democratic Labour Party and a small but organised revolutionary left. This meant that, from the very beginning, the wider left and the working-class struggles that erupted in the 1970s influenced the Women's Liberation Movement and the pro-choice defence of abortion rights in Britain.

The fight to defend the Abortion Act 1967 started as soon as it was enacted. Pro-choice Labour MP Jo Richardson pointed to 12 different attempts to challenge the Abortion Act in an NAC newsletter celebrating the Act's 20-year anniversary (Richardson, 1988). In the past, the main arena for activists had been the corridors of Westminster; but now the law was the property of all, and the struggle to defend it generated a militancy and mobilised numbers on a scale never before seen in support of abortion rights. NAC was militant and confident; as Stephen Brooke (2013, p207) has noted, it 'changed the space of abortion advocacy, from the Central Lobby to the street'. Pro-choice activists originally launched NAC to oppose an amendment by Tory MP James White, a former supporter of the 1967 Act who decided that in his view too many abortions were now taking place. He declared the Act was allowing abortion on demand; he wanted to crack down on access, and won the backing of outright opponents of abortion. But the new political activism confronting the anti-abortion lobby put women's rights at the centre of the debate (Brooke, 2013). The slogan 'a women's right to choose' was taken up, including within ALRA. NAC mobilised feminists politicised through the Women's Liberation Movement and socialists and activists within the labour movement at a time when women were joining trade unions in the highest numbers ever seen. NAC's first national demonstration in 1975 mobilised 20,000 people, and its first conference the same year was 1,000-strong (NAC, 1992, p16).

NAC quickly had 350 groups across Britain. Its slogans fitted the political consciousness of the day. Grassroots activists within the left and feminists in women's groups and the women's movement raised the issue of abortion rights in trade unions, student campuses and campaign groups. The following year, 10,000 took part in another national march. Activist Leonora Lloyd worked for NAC during part of the 1980s, and recalled:

> Many women became involved in abortion politics in the mid 70s, ironically due to the efforts of the anti-abortionists ... We set up the NAC to fight the White Bill in 1975. The renewed activity drew younger women into ALRA also, and led to the Women's Right to Choose Campaign within ALRA. There was no competition between us, as we worked in different ways and attracted different groups of supporters. (Grahame, 1989, p102)

White didn't win, but the pro-choice side continued to grow, and it wasn't long before it had to mobilise again. The fight for abortion rights became part of wider political changes that saw women in every arena, including within the unions and the Labour Party, demanding their voices be heard. Women's rights, inequality and sexual liberation were all on the agenda. The most significant mobilisation in defence of abortion rights came in response to Tory MP John Corrie's attempt to curtail access in 1979. NAC had initiated a campaign to oppose this attack, the Campaign against Corrie, which involved wider forces than those involved in NAC (NAC, 1992). The right to abortion was debated in unions, workplaces and student campuses across the country. One trade unionist described her NALGO branch meeting (the public-sector white-collar union, now part of Unison), in which people voted both to defend the Act and for expanding local abortion services. She also reported on a union meeting at the *Daily Mail* on Fleet Street, which voted 300 to 2 to back a TUC demonstration in the defence of abortion rights (Balfour, 1979). Such meetings, debates and votes were taking place across Britain as activists pushed defending abortion rights onto the agenda right through the trade union movement.

As a result of this groundswell of pressure from below, the TUC agreed to call a demonstration to defend abortion rights in the face of any future attacks. It was quickly asked to deliver on this promise with Corrie's Bill, and called a national demonstration for October 1979. The demonstration was an historic event It was the first time a trade union federation had called a mass demo in support of abortion rights. One feminist historian of the women's movement recognised it as 'the largest trade union demonstration ever held for a cause which lay beyond the traditional scope of collective bargaining; it was also the biggest ever pro abortion march' (Coote and Campbell, p157). It was a tremendous achievement and generated a sense of confidence and resilience against the bigots and reactionaries who had been leading the assaults on abortion rights. Women on the march expressed this mood. Jean Hamilton and Jean Golding, members of the Tobacco Workers' Union who had travelled from Stirling in Scotland, said:

> Sex is no longer something under the table. You discuss it at home with your children. It's on the TV and in the papers. Things are different now. No one is embarrassed and afraid like they used to be. There has been a great change in attitudes. Legal abortion has been an important part of that. We can't go back to the backstreets, to hiding and being ashamed.[31]

The fact that the pro-choice argument was won in the trade union movement, including within unions with solely or predominantly male memberships, was a transforming moment (see interview with Jan Nielsen). Abortion wasn't just out of the backstreet as a procedure; tens of thousands marching through central London chanting their support for a women's right to choose pushed it from being a personal burden of individual women to being firmly out in the open as a social issue:

> As the Corrie Bill progressed through Parliament, labour movement activities continued. Regional trade union conferences on abortion were organised, as were 'weeks of action' in January 1980, which included trade union activity. Two major events were organised for February 1980. A mass lobby and rally on 5 February was called by the CACB [Campaign Against the Corrie Bill] and supported by the South East Regional TUC ... About 12,000 pro-choice activists attended, with thousands queuing in Parliament Square for hours to lobby their MPs. (Hoggart, 2010)

On International Women's Day in 1980, up to 5,000 demonstrated at parliament. It was a period of energetic political activism and debate. Local groups and the national campaigns brought together people with many different political ideas. For example, some women who defined themselves as radical feminists regarded working with the labour movement to defend a flawed Abortion Act as watering down feminist principles and wanted to maintain women-only activity. But in the end, Corrie was beaten because the defence of abortion united hundreds of thousands against the attacks. For many of those who marched in October 1979, the backstreet was still in living memory; they were not going to be forced to return to it. Alongside them was a new generation of activists eager to get stuck into a fight for women's rights in a society rife with sexism and inequality. Access to legal and safe abortion was seen as a class issue that both women and men had an interest in defending. The sheer collective strength of the trade union movement and the scale of the mobilisations were not only critical in beating Corrie but also set back the anti-abortion lobby for years.

The next major attempt to amend the Act was not until 1987, with Liberal MP David Alton's Bill to cut the time limit to 18 weeks. NAC set up Fight the Alton Bill (FAB) to challenge it. Once again, local groups sprung up all over Britain. A march in Glasgow jointly called by the Scottish TUC and FAB saw 3,000 march under more than 70 banners, including trade unions representing firefighters, rail workers, civil service and local government workers. Protests of 300 or more took place in a dozen other cities. The battles of the 1970s showed what could be mobilised in defence of women's rights. They ensured the trade union movement became an important part of the fight for greater access of abortion in Britain for years to come – support that remains strong today.[32]

The anti-abortion side has often been divided. For example, Life deemed SPUC, an extreme anti-abortion group that opposes all abortions, too willing to compromise. Such splits weakened the anti-abortion side on several occasions. SPUC has deep pockets to fund its propaganda, has used every opportunity to push its reactionary views and has backed numerous attempts to challenge or curtail the 1967 Act. It is still at the forefront of opposing access to legal abortion and pumps out a constant stream of anti-abortion propaganda, including in schools; SPUC offered 'education packages' to every secondary school in 2008 as part of a huge anti-abortion propaganda push (Banyard, 2010), and arranges for its representatives to be invited into schools. Research by Education for Choice (2012) has shown that this may be because teachers are sometimes under pressure to provide 'balance' on what are seen as controversial issues. Its study exposed the lies that such speakers have told, including presentations that 'falsely link abortion to cancer, infertility and an invented medical condition called "Post-Abortion Syndrome"'.

Anti-abortion groups have also tried to build support with universities, but have been met with resistance from pro-choice students and the National Union of Students (NUS). The NUS Women's Campaign has worked with the Abortion Rights campaign to fight to keep campuses pro-choice.[33] Leeds Metropolitan University Students' Union created a policy to stop anti-choice campaigners spreading lies about abortion by mandating that materials had to be academically referenced and checked for validity.[34] When anti-choice campaigners visited the University of Cambridge in 2012, the students' union women's campaign protested and brought a bedsheet to cover the large images they used to try to shock students. Birmingham University students have taken part in Stand up for Choice counterprotests in the city against the now annual anti-abortion 'March for Life' mobilisation. In 2017 prochoice protesters including students and trade unionists blocked the 'March for Life' route and demanded Birmingham council refuse permission for an anti-abortion rally to be allowed to take place in the city centre in the future.[35]

In 2008, the Human Fertilisation and Embryology Bill saw anti-choice MPs – headed up by Tory MP Nadine Dorries – put amendments to curtail abortion rights, particularly time limits. Abortion Rights mobilised protests on the ground against the proposed attacks, and pro-choice MPs put amendments to extend abortion rights. These included a move to allow nurses to administer pills and for this to be allowed within GP surgeries – and, most importantly, an amendment to extend abortion rights under the 1967 Act to Northern Ireland. But after months of campaigning and a postponement of the vote over a summer recess, a procedural manoeuvre by the Labour government meant the amendment on Northern Ireland was never discussed. This caused dismay among pro-choice campaigners, who believed it was a unique opportunity to extend abortion rights in Northern Ireland. It is widely accepted (although denied by Gordon Brown at the time) that the Labour leadership did a deal with nine Democratic Unionist Party MPs from Northern Ireland. This deal assured them that Labour would not let abortion rights be extended to Northern Ireland if the MPs supported controversial legislation to extend detention without trial of terror suspects to 42 days, which they did.[36] So, once again, women in Northern Ireland did not win equal access to abortion rights; but at the same time, the anti-abortion lobby was beaten back in its attempts to cut back on rights already won. The threat posed by the possibility of cutting time limits saw pro-choice forces organise on the ground in a way not seen for years.

Despite all the efforts of the anti-abortion lobby, the need for legal and safe abortion has become absorbed into British society. It has become the commonsense for the majority of people – so much so that many are not aware of the actual legislation until they have occasion to be faced with its limitations. British Social

Attitudes surveys have asked questions on views on abortion over several decades. One question they have tracked over time is: 'Do you think the law should allow an abortion when the woman decides on her own she does not wish to have the child'? – which, as the survey points out, is not allowed by the 1967 Act. They found only 37% said 'yes' to this when asked in 1983; by 2012, the proportion answering 'yes' had risen to 62% (Ormston and Curtice, 2015).

But the bedrock of support for legal abortion does not deter the anti-abortion campaigners, who carry on attempting to erode the right to legal and safe abortions. Even where opponents of abortion cannot ban it, or limit it with salami-slice tactics that claim to be making small 'reasonable' changes, they aim to maximise the stigma that surrounds it. They want to ensure abortion continues to be seen as an unsavoury and problematic option for a pregnant woman. The mass 'Women's Marches' of January 2017 and the opposition to the Tories' post-election deal with the anti-abortion DUP show the support that exists for a robust defence of women's rights against the anti-abortion lobby. A generation of young people has no memory of life before access to legal abortion became possible, but has shown they are ready to mobilise in their millions across the globe to assert a woman's right to choose what she does with her body.

SIX

Women's bodies as battlegrounds

Women and their bodies are battlegrounds for society's debates over moral and ideological values – whether that's about women's appearance and behaviour, their sexual activity or even clothes and alcohol consumption. Women's oppression affects every part of women's lives. Today, across the highest ranks of the establishment and state, women are a minority. Only 32% of MPs are women, and in early 2017 only 7% of chief executives in the FTSE 100 Index companies were women. At the top of the judiciary, the imbalance is dramatic; there is only one woman member of the 11-strong Supreme Court.

Yet women's oppression is not simply represented by a 'glass ceiling' blocking elite women from reaching the top. It is also seen in the fact that women form the majority of those on minimum wage. This is referred to as the 'sticky floor' that is holding the majority of women back. Equal pay is still not a reality; despite gains made, the Equal Pay Act 1970 and subsequent Equality Act 2010, the Fawcett Society estimates the current gender pay gap for full-time workers is 13.9%.[1] The inequality of women is built into the very structures of the system.

When it comes to sexuality and fertility, women's reproductive rights are under constant scrutiny (Criado-Perez, 2015). This condemnation can include selfish 'career' women without children, teenage mothers, lesbian mums or women trying to access in vitro fertilisation (IVF) treatment on the NHS. Women in powerful positions also suffer discrimination and sexist behaviour – oppression cuts across the class divide. For example, a meeting between two powerful politicians, Prime Minster Theresa May and Scottish First Minister Nicola Sturgeon, in March 2017, was reported on the front page of national newspaper the *Daily Mail* with a full-length photo of the two women. The headline was 'Never mind Brexit, who won Legs-it!'[2] May was also forced to go public about her inability to have children by Tory leadership challenger Andrea Leadsom, who implied May couldn't have a real stake in the future of Britain because she was not a mother.[3] But Theresa May went on to win the highest office in the government, and her experience is very different to that of the majority of women. She and fellow wealthy and powerful women show scant solidarity with women who do not have the same resources to overcome discriminatory hurdles. Before she went to meet US President Donald Trump for the first time May stated she would not take up his misogynist statements and policies claiming that the very fact that she was a female political leader was challenge enough.[4] Her presence in the White House holding hands (literally and metaphorically) with Trump would hardly have been a comfort for the millions of ordinary women in the US facing a wholesale assault on their reproductive rights.[5]

Why does abortion matter so much?

The view of women as mothers and carers is deeply embedded in the way society is organised, as well as within its institutions, traditions and ideology. It is both imposed and often internalised by women as the norm to which they should adhere and in which they will find ultimate fulfilment. Journalist Caitlin Moran (2011) has, unusually for a public figure, written about having an abortion and why she has no regrets about it. She points out that abortions are so rarely seen as a 'positive thing' because: 'Our view of motherhood is still so idealised and misty – Mother, gentle giver of life – that the thought of a mother subsequently setting limits on her capacity to nurture, and refusing to give further life, seems obscene' (Moran, 2011, p272). In fact, as Sally Sheldon shows, even the way abortion law has been approached reveals 'the assumption of maternity as the female norm' because a legal abortion is allowed if another pregnancy might negatively affect a woman's ability to be a good mother to already existing children (Sheldon, 1997, p43).

Such views of abortion as a rejection of natural womanhood have been seen historically. For example, one Medical Officer of Health complained in 1905 that the use of abortifacients during pregnancy was 'a false conception of the obligations of matrimony' (Hall, 2013, p39). A decade later, a correspondent in a study of birthrates (see Chapter Three) wrote of women attempting to abort their pregnancies: 'there is involved a terrible indifference or contempt for motherhood' (Elderton, 1914, p140). Such ideas flow from the whole way society is organised around assumptions about what women's caring role will be. The world of work and its maternity and paternity leave and pay make gender roles difficult to break. Today dominant ideology about women's role in society maintains the stereotype of women's main sphere being the home and family. While this does not fit the reality of women's lives, the ideas still serve a purpose; they help make women feel that although they work outside the home, work inside the home is still something for which they have to be largely responsible. All this still shapes discussion of women's reproductive choices, helping create much of the stigma that still surrounds abortion today.

The ideology of what was 'natural' and 'acceptable' behaviour for women in the early 1960s was so dominant that even some who supported women's right to abortion made moral judgements and differentiated between deserving and undeserving women. Married women with many children were deserving; someone sleeping around for fun was not. Up until the late 1960s, the difference between attitudes to married and unmarried women was entrenched in British prevailing ideas and medical practice. Such prejudices partly explain how terms evolved such as 'family planning' in Britain and 'Planned Parenthood' in the US. These imply that contraception is solely about controlling *when* and *how* – not *whether* – to have children. These formulations were an attempt to make birth control and abortion 'respectable', and to say: 'don't worry – we will have a family, we just want to plan it better'.

The model family

The institution of the modern nuclear family has gone through many changes over generations. But a model of the nuclear family remains the ideal to be aspired to within popular culture, in movies and magazines and TV adverts, and by politicians and religious leaders. Despite the many glowing images of happy couples and laughing children sharing a meal around a table, the real family is a contradictory place; it can be a haven and a hell. Within the family, you can find love and support and intimate ties that bind and offer solidarity. But you can also find dashed hopes and frustrations, domestic violence and abuse and repressive expectations that alienate family members from each other.

There is no doubting the important role the family plays in the eyes of the establishment. It is seen as helping to maintain stability, and encourages people to conform to society's expectations. It teaches self-reliance, gender roles and deference to authority. We are told that it's our responsibility to take care of the next generation, the elderly and the sick – not society's. If a young person doesn't get a decent education or job, if they have to eat meals donated from a foodbank or go to school hungry, it is seen as the responsibility of individual families – not the system. Family responsibility was even enforced by the courts for a time under the Poor Law, passed in 1601. This legally obliged family members to take responsibility for each other. Parents had to take care of children, and when the children were grown up they became legally responsible for their parents. Many working-class people did not need to be told to care for their families by the law; the bonds of kin were enough to motivate them to do all they could to support fellow family members in hard times (Roberts, 1984). But the law was about imposing the importance of family responsibility – as if a lack of it was what was causing people's impoverishment.

Families in which men brought home wages and women made a caring and clean home were seen as the model during the majority of the 20th century. This model was increasingly put under pressure by the explosion of numbers of women joining the expanding workforce during the postwar boom.

When families 'broke down', it was women who got the blame. Working mothers were told that their 'latchkey' children – so called because they had to let themselves into their homes after school – were in danger of becoming 'juvenile delinquents'.[6] This was supposedly because of the neglect such children were said to experience. Alongside the important ideological role the family plays in modern capitalism is a heavy economic burden. Tory Prime Minister Margaret Thatcher once acknowledged the dual role she saw the family as playing when she told a conference of Tory women in 1988 that it:

> is the building block of society … It encompasses the whole of society. It fashions our beliefs. It is the preparation for the rest of our life ... It is a nursery, it is a school, a hospital, a leisure centre, a place of refuge and a place of rest … and women run it. (Seal, 1990, p73)

More recently in November 2015, Tory Prime Minister David Cameron echoed this view, saying in parliament: 'families are the best welfare state that we have, they bring up our children, they teach us the right values and they care for us when we are sick and unwell'.[7] Right-wing politicians often eulogise the family to facilitate their dismantling of the welfare state. This is frequently combined with stigmatising anyone reliant on benefits. Tory politicians encourage voters to make moral judgements between 'strivers and skivers'. Television crews make documentaries about poor and unemployed people as if they are studying another species on a wildlife programme. Poverty is spun as a bad lifestyle choice that responsible people can avoid.

Shoring up the model of the nuclear family, even when it doesn't fit with women's and men's lives today, is as important as ever. It is about maintaining a situation in which the majority of people are encouraged to get by with the least possible cost to the state. These views have been most vigorously pushed in the years since the financial crash of 2008. They are used to legitimise austerity drives that intensify the economic burden carried by individual working-class families. Whatever the rhetoric, cuts in living standards mean life has become harder for women and men who want to have children. They are faced with unaffordable housing, and the woman is faced with the prospect of losing her salary – and even her job – if she takes time out to have a baby. The TUC *Motherhood Pay Penalty Report* in 2016 found that: 'By the age of 42, mothers who are in full-time work are earning 11% less than fulltime women without children'.[8] Instead of well-resourced nursery provision and generous maternity and paternity benefits, mothers face systematic discrimination. One 2014 study revealed that more than 40% of managers say they are wary of employing women of childbearing age, or who already had children, and one third prefer to employ men in their twenties and thirties to avoid paying out for maternity leave.[9]

In 2016, the Women and Equalities Committee reported evidence that: 'In 2005, 30,000 women lost their jobs as a result of pregnancy discrimination. The first findings in 2015 showed that 54,000 women lost their jobs as a result of pregnancy discrimination'.[10] Families are also expected to fill the gaps created by the growing crisis in social care provision for the elderly, cuts to respite care for parents looking after disabled or sick children and support for disabled people to live their lives independently.[11] Those women who do wait to try to gain some financial and career security before they have children may find it harder to get pregnant. It's not just the Japanese government that has introduced egg freezing; in the US, several of the big IT firms (including Facebook and Google) now offer this procedure for women workers in their pay and perks packages to help them get pregnant later in their career.[12] One company in the US runs fashionable parties coined 'Let's Chill' in which women drink free cocktails, nibble canapés and hear from doctors about the procedure – which one company 'run by women for women' describes as 'empowering', and which can cost up to $10,000.[13] Even if this were a desirable option, it is out of reach for most women.

The institution of marriage

Motherhood is seen as an instinctive role for women, but until the late 1960s and 1970s this supposedly 'natural' role was only to be fulfilled if they had a marriage certificate. In fact, procreation was referred to as the first reason for marriage in the Christian *Book of Common Prayer's* traditional marriage vows. Women were expected to not only have children but also be responsible for the whole domestic sphere in the privatised family. Without the official legal and religious recognition of marriage, sexual activity was deemed immoral and motherhood a shameful state. It may be difficult for younger generations to fully appreciate the impact of becoming an 'unmarried mother' in the 1950s and 1960s, when your children would be defined as 'illegitimate'. Men were never described as 'unmarried fathers'. Denise's description of women being told they would lose their reputation if they had a baby when unmarried is an example of the pressure on women to fulfil the role as keepers of their chastity and purity (see interview with Denise). A woman was not just made to feel personal shame; the stigma was such that she was also made to feel responsible for bringing shame on her whole family.

Because only sexual activity between heterosexual married couples was seen as legitimate, when early family planning services were launched, for a time only these couples were allowed to access contraception (Paintin, 1998). The services were not created to enable healthy active sex lives without the worry of unwanted pregnancy; they were about planning well-spaced, healthy families. So, when local authorities were told in 1930 they could choose to offer contraceptive services, this was only to be offered to 'married women for whom further pregnancy would be a health hazard'. Dorothy Limbrick worked at the Birmingham Brook Advisory Centre when it was first launched, and recalls why blocking contraceptive services to unmarried people made the service necessary:

> The whole reason that it was set up was because the Family Planning Association [FPA] couldn't cope with the demand from people who were not married because they only saw married people. The FPA had widened their group to people who were engaged and therefore about to be married (which involved a lot of young women going to Woolworths and buying rings and then coming back and saying they were engaged). (Limbrick, 2014)

It was only in 1964 that London County Council decided to 'extend the giving of family planning advice to unmarried people' (Fryer, 1965, p269). So, the choices available to women who got pregnant accidentally as a result of being denied access to reliable contraception were to have a backstreet abortion and risk the consequences, get married and have the baby or carry the pregnancy and give the baby up for adoption. Figures show that many couples did opt for a fast marriage: 'In 1960, 27% of first births were less than eight months after the date of the marriage (this proportion decreased progressively in the 1970s to become negligible in the 1980s)' (Paintin, 1998, p12).

Those women who could not or would not marry but longed to keep their baby were often denied that chance. Many were sent to 'mother and baby' homes for unmarried mothers, where women report feeling pressured to give their child up for adoption; others simply had their babies taken away. Some estimates are that as many as half a million babies went through such an adoption process, run by churches and The Salvation Army in Britain from the 1950s to the 1970s (Sherwood, 2016). Local authorities in Britain only took over responsibility for adoption services in 1976. Today, many of the women whose babies were taken from them are lobbying the government to open a public enquiry into such adoptions.

Veronica Smith, co-founder of the Movement for an Adoption Apology, has taken up campaigning and speaking out about her own experience; she gave birth to a daughter in 1964 who was taken from her to be adopted.[14] Veronica is now 75 years old, yet she says the event 'has coloured the whole of my life'.[15] She wants to speak out, but she knows that many other women who have gone through the same experience find that impossible, even decades later:

> But there are lots of women who can't even verbalise what happened to them. They are screwed up with pain and shame and guilt. There are thousands who have never come forward, but every time there is publicity on this people make contact wanting to tell their story, often for the first time.[16]

The notion of the 'fallen woman' had been enshrined in law in 1913 with the Mental Deficiency Act, which empowered local authorities to 'certify women who were homeless, destitute or, in official eyes, "immoral" and detain them indefinitely' (Humphries, 1989, p64). Lucy Bland points out that the Act meant moral deficiency was 'recast in medical terms' (2002, p242). This legitimised the most reactionary policies that punished women who broke from society's restrictive views of their role. When the law changed, it was too late for those women who had become institutionalised – even though when they were first incarcerated they had no mental health problems. All they had done was give birth outside marriage. One such woman, who journalist Stephen Humphries interviewed for a television documentary in the 1980s, had been locked up for a half a century (Humphries, 1989).

Women who became pregnant outside of marriage were also forced into religious institutions, Catholic and Protestant. In Ireland and Britain, young women were sent to work in laundries and other institutions after they had given birth, the most infamous being the Magdalene Laundries. Most never found out what happened to their babies after they were taken away. Some were sold to rich couples, some as far away as in the US. Papers released by Ireland's Foreign Office in early 2017 suggest that around ten babies were sent every month in the 1950s to the US from Ireland for adoption.[17] The Irish state and Catholic Church colluded to ensure the babies were speedily issued with passports to enable them to travel.[18] The discovery, in February 2017, of the remains of babies and children buried in a mass grave at the site of a Bon Secours Mother and Baby Home, run by Catholic nuns in Tuam in the West of Ireland, indicates what may have been the fate of others.[19]

As if the brutal treatment of women in such institutions was not bad enough, the ideology around them was all about the guilt of women. For example, the Ulster Magdalene Asylum on the Donegall Pass in central Belfast described itself as: 'For the reception of erring and repentant females'.[20] Some women who gave birth outside marriage were placed in actual prisons. In Belfast, the Ulster Female Penitentiary in Brunswick Street, established in 1839, described itself as a 'noble institution' that 'receives penitent victims of seduction and encourages them to work for their own support within the walls of the Institution, where there are the most extensive and appropriate facilities for washing, drying, mangling &c' (note that even when acknowledged as victims, women must be penitent).[21] Some estimates suggest that in the 20th century alone, 30,000 women went through such laundries. The last Magdalene Laundry closed its doors only in 1996. The true legacy of such places and the brutality of both physical and sexual abuse they bred is still being revealed by survivors' tenacious fight for justice.[22]

Ireland has a particularly grim history when it comes to the treatment of women's bodies. All aspects of women's bodily autonomy have been affected by oppressive attitudes and structures relating to women's fertility. For example, symphysiotomy – a brutal method to deliver babies, originating in the 19th century – was resurrected in 1940s Ireland for difficult births, driven by the belief that all women should have a large number of children.[23] This procedure involved severing pelvic joints, and in some cases using a hacksaw to break the pubic bone in women who were having trouble giving birth. The women not only suffered indescribable pain but also, in many cases, lifelong health problems. This operation was used on over 1,500 women over five decades. It was an unnecessary procedure carried out without consent – and in many cases without the woman being fully informed even afterwards. Women who survived this barbaric practice started a campaign in 2016 to win compensation, and are still demanding restitution.[24] The women say doctors didn't want to deliver their babies by caesarian section as there was a belief that it was unsafe for a woman to have more than three caesarians. In a society that glorified childbearing, a symphysiotomy was seen as an alternative to a procedure that might limit a woman's ability to bear more children. The horror of what the Church and state has inflicted on women over decades in Ireland has created a toxic legacy of shame and suffering that survived through generations.

Today, whether women are married or not is thankfully no longer an issue, although most birth certificates do include a father's name. Yet, as previously mentioned, single parents, the vast majority of whom are mothers, are still a favoured target for moral judgement and financial penalty. The way the media portrays working-class women in general reveals much about society's attitudes; working-class and poor women face the most relentless censure. Moral panics in Britain have been whipped up about 'feral' young people on council estates, teenagers getting pregnant to get housing and binge-drinking women out on the lash on a Friday night. An *Edinburgh Evening News* piece from 2004 is a typical caricature; the journalist describes 'slack-jawed girls with enough gold or gold-plated jewellery to put H Samuel out of business. They are the dole-scroungers, petty criminals, football hooligans and teenage pram-pushers' (Tyler, 2008, p24). Compare this to the words of the Tory Shadow Minister for Health in 1974: 'the balance of our population, our human stock is threatened ... a recent article ... showed that a high and rising proportion of children are being born to mothers least fitted to bring children into the world and bring them up' (Greenwood and Young, 1976, p95). We have moved a long way from the crude eugenics dominant a century ago. But remnants of the ideas that working-class and poor people are morally weak and undermine the racial stock of British society, and that working-class women's sexuality has to be controlled, have persevered.

Women are morally judged as responsible for any unplanned pregnancy. It is presumed it was the woman's responsibility to avoid it. Even the famous legal case prompted by the abortion carried out by pro-law-reform doctor Aleck Bourne in 1938 shows the impact of such deep-rooted prejudices. Bourne believed abortion should be legalised, and took up the case of a 14-year-old girl who had suffered multiple rape by a group of soldiers. He recalled in his memoirs that before he agreed to carry out the abortion he put the girl in a ward under observation for eight days:

> to be sure of the type of girl I was dealing with. Many of the prostitute type or those of low intelligence are completely untroubled by pregnancy, except that for the first of these groups it is an obvious nuisance but nothing more. The mentally retarded girl is usually if not always, entirely indifferent to her condition. (Potts et al, 1977, p288)

Then, when he had to do an internal examination:

> The occasion caused a complete breakdown of her morale. All her assumed cheerfulness disappeared as she wept beyond control. This decided me at once that she had to be relieved of her pregnancy. In her there was nothing of the cold indifference of the prostitute. (Hindell and Simms, 1971, p70)

The case is now better remembered for the fact that it set a new legal precedent (pointed out in Chapter Two). It is chilling to think that this girl may have been refused an abortion, even from a relatively sympathetic doctor for the time, if she had continued to appear 'cheerful'.

When anti-abortion campaigners today decry the supposed ease with which women can get abortions in Britain, or claim women are having 'quickie' abortions in their lunch breaks,[25] it is part of the same agenda. They reveal their distaste for women who don't appear to feel guilt and trauma about having an abortion. Presumably they would prefer to see women suffer more and for longer to pay for their 'waywardness'. Such interventions ensure it is more difficult for women to feel comfortable with making a choice to end an unwanted pregnancy. In the past, anti-abortion doctors have punished women by denying them pain relief during a termination – as described by two of this book's interviewees. Jane McKay, a former Secretary of Glasgow TUC, described her experience of having a legal abortion in the early 1970s: 'Many women including myself were in absolute pain after the termination but really didn't receive the appropriate medication'. She was only given proper pain relief when a relative happened to come on duty as the Sister on the ward. Ann Rossiter describes how she ended up in a London hospital after a botched backstreet abortion in the 1960s: 'the medical staff were far from welcoming … I was in a fog of pain which they didn't do much to alleviate'. (See interviews with Jane McKay and Ann Rossiter.)

Working-class women seeking abortions have sometimes been subjected to brutal experimentation as a form of punishment. During the 19th century, one Lancashire doctor was willing to perform abortions on women whose bodies had developed some sort of physical impediment as a result of factory work (McLaren, 1977). But if they came back a second time, the only termination he would carry out was a (largely untested) caesarean section. This was both a form of punishment and a way of developing techniques using women whose lives and bodies were considered of little value. Historian Angus McLaren (1977, p76) writes that: 'Of the 55 caesarians performed in Britain before 1880 twenty five took place in the factory districts of Lancashire'. He also discovered that only two women survived these operations: one died in childbirth when she next became pregnant; the other, 31 years old at the time of the operation, was left paralysed and lived for only another four years (McLaren, 1977).

Sexuality

The censorious view of women's sexuality is sometimes hidden, sometimes open. But striving for everyone to be able to enjoy free expression of their sexuality has to be a part of any vision for women's liberation. Lucy Bland has explored the contradictions in how women's sexuality has been portrayed historically; women have been regarded as both naturally chaste, but also as dangerous temptresses to be controlled (Bland, 2002). In *Girl Trouble*, Carol Dyhouse similarly argues that young women are invariably either portrayed as 'victims or sluts' (2013, p182). Women who enjoy sex or are open about their sexual desires are judged immoral, while men who do the same are lauded as 'studs'.

Arguments about morality, women's pleasure and sexual liberation are not just an invention of the 1960s, nor even the 20th century. The Victorian view of women's sexuality as entirely passive is in contradiction to some earlier views of fertility that saw women's sexual pleasure as essential to procreation. There was a time when women's enjoyment of sex was central to ideas about fertility and 'acknowledged and valued' (McLaren, 1984, p146). The link between greater enjoyment of sex and lifting the fear of unwanted pregnancy was described by George Drysdale, author of a bestselling account of contraception published in 1854. He argued:

> women if they had not the fear of becoming pregnant before their eyes would indulge their sexual desires just as men do. Hence the vehement prejudices in favour of our present code of sexual morality, and of the institution of marriage, together with the determined hostility to anything in the shape of unmarried intercourse, at least on the part of women. (Fryer, 1965, p112)

When birth control campaigner Marie Stopes published her handbook for couples, *Married Love,* in 1918, it provoked horror among some commentators. For example, they condemned her suggestion that 'women may embrace men with their legs as well as their arms' in case it suggested activity that most women wouldn't otherwise be aware of. It became a bestseller (Fryer, 1965, p226). The quest for sex for enjoyment and not simply for procreation has led to some debates about the nature of women's sexuality among modern-day feminists. Looking back at the late 1960s, some – such as Germaine Greer – argued that the 'sexual revolution', alongside the development of the pill and access to abortion, in the end mainly benefited men. In Greer's view, women 'lost the right to say no': 'Once they had made the investment in sexual activity by taking a daily medication in order to be available, there was no sense in being unavailable' and men were able to have sex with whom they wanted without any consequences.[26] But this is an inversion of the benefits of the liberalising of sexual habits. Winning sexual liberation was a fundamental part of the Women's Liberation Movement. Women fought for the right to express their sexuality without being judged and without punishment. It was always women – particularly working-class women – who suffered the harshest consequences of unwanted pregnancies, and so they had the most to gain from the opening up of access to all forms of birth control. But such arguments show how enduring the idea that women can't enjoy their sexuality really is.

We have seen that most early advocates of birth control and abortion argued from the point of view of women who had an unbearable burden of giving birth to too many children, or lived in severe poverty making them unable to support large families (see Chapter Three). Those such as Stella Browne, who advocated preventing or ending unwanted pregnancies as a women's right to enjoy their sexuality, were always a minority. Browne said she supported the right to abortion: 'The right (as yet still rather unpopular an assumption) that women are really human beings, and that freedom of choice and deliberate intention are necessary for them in their sexual relations and their maternity if they are to make anything of their status and opportunities in certain communities today' (Hall, 2011, pp207-208).

Challenges to the social and sexual mores imposed on the majority from above – though rarely adhered to by their advocates – have been a feature of periods of profound social upheaval. Before the revolts and social movements of the 1960s, such changes took place during the Great Depression of the 1930s, and (as previously described) during the First and Second World Wars. The revolutionary wave across Europe that started in Russia in 1917 saw the most dramatic challenges to the status quo. The Russian Revolution, kicked off by women workers marching on International Women's Day, saw the fall of the Tsarist dictatorship and within months the creation of a workers' government (Cliff, 1978). As in every great social struggle, the question of women's role, the family and sexuality came to the fore after generations of living under a repressive regime (McDermid & Hillyar, 1999). Central to the challenge of winning women's equality was the need for women to be liberated from the material oppression of backbreaking work in the home. But it was also seen as a priority for women to be liberated from endless childbearing. The Soviet Union became the first country to legalise abortion on demand in 1920, as well as to decriminalise homosexuality and to allow both women and men to instigate divorce on demand.

The reality of women's position in a country devastated by years of war and then an attempted counterrevolution by the old order should not be romanticised. Yet the achievement was significant, and brought in laws not seen in the West for a further 50 years. A discussion at one doctors' conference in 1932 reveals the debates of the time, as a Dr Zelinsky responded to some delegates' objections to the free availability of abortion:

> One of the speakers here exclaimed in horror: 'All that is needed is the certificate of the doctor and the desire of the woman, and there you have an abortion'. Yes, that is exactly the way it should be; the desire of the women is sufficient, because the right to determine the social indications for abortion is the woman's and nobody else's. None among us men would tolerate it if some commission or other had the say about our marriage, if they, according to their social concepts, could consent to our getting married or veto it. So, don't keep the woman from deciding the cardinal question of life for herself. The woman has a right to a sexual life and wants to realise it just as a man does, and if she wants to be a full social and biological being, she must have the fullest possibilities of realising it. (Widgery, 1975)

Tragically, the hopes and dreams of October 1917 were defeated by the rise of Stalinism before they were fully realised. Stalin wanted women to become the breeders of the next generation of workers to help build the Soviet Union to compete with the West in the new Cold War. Women were given medals for their seventh and following children to encourage large families, and from 1936 abortion was heavily restricted once again (Rosenberg, 1999).

Ideas and action

We will only be able to fully sweep away the ideology surrounding the legal and moral judgements of women's lives when society is shaped by the needs of the majority – not the other way around. That means free access to contraception and abortion, as well as an end to discrimination against women who do have children. Women should not face a financial penalty for taking time out to have children. Offering egg freezing for women in the workplace may be a provision that some women will want to take up, but it does not offer a solution to unequal pay and systemic discrimination. Rather than women and men being forced to bend to the demands of the world of work, it's time that work and society are moulded to fit around the real lives of women and men. Women's role in society cannot be confined or defined by their potential ability to have children.

SEVEN

What we need

> Abortion ... should be available for any woman, without insolent inquisitions, nor ruinous financial charges, nor tangles or red tape. For our bodies are our own. (Stella Browne, in Rowbotham, 1977, p114)

It's well into the 21st century, so why are we still having to talk about abortion and reproductive rights? Why can't free contraception and abortion care be available to all women, regardless of income, geography or background? Why does class define what access we have to health and reproductive services? How can choice be exercised when faced with poverty, racism and inequality?

These are just some of the questions this book has tried to address. But this final chapter is about looking at how things could be different; about what the future could look like. So much pro-choice activism around abortion rights over the last 50 years in the US and Britain has by necessity been defensive. Is has been a fight to stop the Right rowing back on gains made in the past. Defending current provision from attack is vital; without vigilance, anti-abortion campaigners in Britain would have beaten back many rights we have won. The experience of the US shows that reforms won in the past cannot be taken for granted and that even with technical legality, without guarantees of access women are still denied their rights.

Abortion rights in Britain could be massively transformed very easily. Here are just a few steps that could be implemented straight away.

Remove abortion from the criminal law

Abortion needs to be decriminalised. There is absolutely no justification for this common and safe medical procedure within women's health care to be governed by criminal law – let alone a law that was passed in parliament the century before last, when women couldn't even vote, let alone stand for parliament. If abortion was removed from criminal law it would still be governed by medical guidelines and recommendations for best practice, just like all aspects of health care are currently. But the difference would be that these would be decided solely based on what is best for women, not on how to keep within antiquated legislation. So, for example, one very simple intervention would be to abolish the restrictions that force women to return to 'approved premises' to take a second pill for a medical abortion. The BMA called for complete decriminalisation of abortion at their annual conference in June 2017 and the Royal College of Midwives (RCM) also supports this position:

> the RCM does not believe it is right that in the 21st century it is still the case that women who choose to have an abortion can be criminalised and jailed. Accordingly the RCM believes that abortion should be removed from the criminal law.The RCM believes that if we are to be advocates for women then we must advocate for choice on all aspects of their care. This is not about being for or against abortion; it is about being for women and respecting their choices about their bodies.[1]

Just because a woman is pregnant does not mean she has lost her capacity for making decisions about her life and body. The requirement that not just one but two doctors have to approve the validity of every request for an abortion robs women of their autonomy and reflects the paternalist views of the past. Patients' ability to make decisions about their health care is taken for granted in other situations. Women should be able to request an abortion and receive advice and support from medical staff without surrendering the right to make their own decisions. We need to dispose of a law that still insists that two doctors have to sign off on every routine abortion even though in many cases nurses and other medical staff can and do carry out consultations and care, and know best what their patients need.

Deliver abortion care free in an integrated NHS service

The experience of the US shows the dangers of women's reproductive care being left to the mercy of privatised insurers and different state laws. But even in England and Wales, where provision is mainly free to women, only 34% of abortions took place in 2013 in NHS clinics while private providers carry out the majority (Astbury-Ward, 2015). This is in sharp contrast to Scotland, where in 2013 only 40 women out of 12,447 (0.3%) were not treated within an NHS hospital (Astbury-Ward, 2015). As doctors providing abortion care indicate, dependence on private providers ghettoises the service for patients and doctors. It means that doctors originally trained in the NHS who work for private providers become specialists, while within the NHS doctors in women's health care develop little experience of abortion provision. As Dr Tracey Mathews, a consultant in sexual and reproductive health and an abortion care provider, points out: 'Many people, even within women's health care, will be surprised at how common abortion is … They don't see abortion nowadays because it is separated' (see interview with Dr Tracey Matthews).

Make it free for everyone

All contraception and abortion services should be free and widely available to all. Today you can buy the morning after pill over the counter at a pharmacy, but it will cost at least £22 – more than four times the price for the same medication in France. As we have seen free provision of abortion has covered women from Northern Ireland having abortions in Britain from June 2017. But this means women will still be reliant on organisations such as the Abortion Support Network to help them fund their travel, or a bucket will go around working-class pubs in Derry (in echoes of the 19th-century factory abortion club) 'for a woman who needs the fare for Liverpool'. No one asks what for; they all know.

Eliminate delays

Women need to be able to get a prompt appointment when they discover they are pregnant and want to request an abortion. Delays take place because women may come up against waiting times, uncooperative doctors and stretched NHS services. This becomes all the more critical if – for a host of reasons such as age, health history or lack of symptoms – women discover their pregnancy later. Many delays would be avoided without the hurdles and unnecessary bureaucracy that the law has created.

What about time limits?

Many countries across Europe provide abortion on request up to or around 12 weeks of pregnancy, which would be a major improvement on today's situation in Britain. But early abortion on request cannot be brought in at the expense of access after the first 12 weeks. Of course, the vast majority of abortions in Britain take place within this time limit, but the minority that take place after 20 weeks (for example) should not be outlawed. There can be no tradeoff of making earlier abortions more freely available in return for restricting those after that time limit. As has been shown, later abortions often involve women in the most difficult situations, as well as women forced to travel from Ireland (who have to raise funds, arrange flights and leave) and women in parts of the country where access is poor. These women would suffer the most from any attacks on the time limit.

Medical advances

There are medical possibilities that cannot even be properly explored because of the legal situation in Britain. Researchers have put forward suggestions for medication that women could take during each menstrual cycle to ensure a pregnancy is not established. Sally Sheldon (2015) describes the possibilities offered by new medication that acts to end a pregnancy at a very early stage –before or after a fertilised egg has implanted in the wall of the womb. She describes the increasingly blurred line created by such medication that acts to prevent and halt pregnancy, perhaps even before a woman knows or confirms she is pregnant. But she points out how such medication comes up against a 'regulatory cliff edge'.[2] This is because before implantation such medication (including the morning after pill) is treated as a contraceptive, but after implantation the pregnancy is judged to have started and any medication interfering with it is deemed an abortifacient – and therefore controlled by the stringent abortion legislation. So, the law as it stands prevents certain developments that could offer a flexible, early and safe option for women to control their fertility (Sheldon, 2015).

'No more shame, silence, stigma'

This has been one of the chants on pro-choice demonstrations demanding the repeal of the Eighth Amendment in Ireland. Changing the law to make abortion legal and available on request is a vital first step. The history of the control, regulation and stigmatisation of women's fertility, bodies and sexuality has left a legacy. So, as many activists and writers have pointed out, even with decriminalisation there will still be a battle to challenge the stigma that surrounds abortion. As we have seen, this is bound up with women's role in wider society, which shapes assumptions of what our priorities and responsibilities should be.

A mass public information campaign using every form of media is needed to normalise abortion and highlight the fact that it is an everyday part of life that one in three women will go through. At the moment, everyday depictions in the media are overwhelmingly negative, as a year-long study of British newspapers over 2010 found; it pointed out that abortion was usually framed as: 'at odds with norms of femininity. Voices of women who have sought abortions were marginalised, with women's reasons for seeking abortion at worst disregarded, and at best over-simplified', while few mentions of abortion framed it as a 'legitimate' choice. (Purcell et al., 2014, p1153). Changing the media and public perceptions is important because women are taught to think of themselves through such perceptions, and can internalise the shame society tells them they should feel if they choose to have an abortion.

Marva Sadler, Director of Clinical Services for Whole Woman's Health in Texas, has described how important the whole atmosphere in the clinic is to challenging stigma. She says that when women come in, they are surprised that it is cheerful and everyone is talking in their normal voices: 'They say "Oh it's so bright in here", or "Everybody's smiling, everybody's so happy" … They expect us to whisper because it's supposed to be a secret and they don't want anybody to know'.[3] Projects such as 'Shout your Abortion', which encourage women to be open about their abortions, and the women who tweet or post their abortion experiences on YouTube are about breaking this 'silence'.[4] But if women everywhere are going to have the confidence to talk about their abortion without fear of moral judgement, we're going to need fundamental changes in how women and their bodies are treated in society.

Sex

Abortion and birth control can't be looked at in vacuum, given that pregnancy is usually a product of sexual activity. Women's bodies and sexuality have long been commodified in modern capitalism – used to advertise everything from tyres to chocolate – but today we are meant to *revel* in our objectification. Women are told our bodies and appearance are our most valuable currency; they are often referred to as women's 'assets'. Today, open and crude sexism is being sold to us as sexual liberation. This plays into the myth that women are now equal and all the old battles have been won. We're not meant to complain if we are treated as sex objects; instead, we're told to see it as just a bit of 'ironic' fun. Commercial sex has never been more in your face online, in shops and in the media. Yet what about the messy business of real sex?

In contrast to the brash and explicit promotion of commercial sex, repressive attitudes that run deep in British society block open discussion of real sexual relationships. This is played out in arguments about the right of school students to a decent sex education. Many young people growing up are denied the opportunity to take part in an open discussion at school about real sexual relations between individuals, over and above the ability to put a condom on a banana or avoid sexually transmitted diseases and unwanted pregnancy. When commentators complain about it being too easy for young people to access porn on mobile phones, the answer isn't a crackdown and censorship; it is to encourage wider open discussion of sex and relationships. After years of campaigning, the Tory government finally agreed in March 2017 to update sex education advice and make it compulsory in all schools in England. Until then in England, only local-authority-funded secondary schools were obliged to offer pupils sex and relationships education (SRE) classes; the majority (65%) of secondary schools that are academies and free schools were under no such obligation. There are now calls for similar moves in the devolved education sectors in Scotland and Wales.[5] Schools in Northern Ireland must offer Relationship and Sexuality Education but the information students receive is not uniform and schools only need deliver what they believe is appropriate for the 'ethos ' of the school. Open and sympathetic sex education is vital for all school students and needs to be delivered by well-trained, confident, unembarrassed staff. Young people themselves have demanded these changes; a YouGov poll commissioned by the children's charity Barnardo's in 2017 found that 70% of 11 to 15 year olds thought SRE should be compulsory.[6]

But it's not just about open discussion among young people. We have seen that women's reproductive health has long been shrouded in taboo and secrecy across society. One of the advances made by the Women's Liberation Movement of the 1960s and 1970s was to bring discussion about women's bodies, sexuality and reproductive choices out in the open. But there is still a long way to go. The fact that abortion is still treated as virtually unmentionable even among women who have had terminations shows that these issues still affect how women feel about their bodies and choices.

Stop meddling

Politicians who want to meddle with women's reproductive choices should be reminded that they are not being asked to have abortions. They are just being asked not to impose their views on women who want and need to have abortions. Decriminalisation of abortion, along with the latest medical advances, has the potential to open up a whole new era in abortion provision and make a real difference in women's lives. But of course, the fight for women to be recognised as more than living incubators is only part of the picture that needs changing in a society riven with division and inequality. In Britain, 28% of children live in poverty – that's over 3.9 million children.[7] According to the US Census Bureau in 2015 almost one in five children in the US live in poverty — that's 15.5 million children. Such statistics and the reality of the lives that lie beneath them are rarely a concern of the hypocrites who make up the anti-abortion camp. They spend millions fighting to force women to have babies, but direct remarkably little outrage at the policies that consign so many already-born children to a bleak future. Donald Trump brags about his gag order blocking international aid to organisations that offer abortion services, but is silent about the millions of already-born babies and children who die due to lack of basic means to live. WHO figures show that every minute a newborn baby dies from infection caused by a lack of safe water and an unclean environment.[8] Shouldn't we have some laws preventing that avoidable and terrible loss of life?

This not a technical issue. We live in a world that sent a man into space way back in 1961 and to the moon in 1969 and launched the Voyager 1 spacecraft in 1977, which is now heading beyond our solar system. So getting clean water and supplies, and for that matter contraceptives and abortion care, to every area of the globe is not a problem of technology or logistics. It's political. Some lives don't matter as much others.

We need to build a fight against all those who want to wage war on women's rights, wherever they are. Everyone can do something. If you're in Britain, join Abortion Rights; elsewhere, look up your local pro-choice organisation (the 'Get Involved' section at the end of this book lists some of these). Get involved.

The anti-abortionists only dominate when the majority stay silent or stay at home. Trump's election has provoked a wave of resistance against his policies, but a movement to stop attacks on women's rights can become a movement *for* an alternative. We should celebrate every expression of defiance against all that's rotten in the world, but at the same time create a positive vision of the sort of society in which we would like to live.

We need a world in which no woman dies because she had to go through a backstreet abortion – or because, like Ann Lovell, she felt she had nowhere to turn and gave birth alone in the street. We need a world in which birth control is not imposed or removed by state diktat but that women and men decide for themselves. We need a society in which poverty and exploitation no longer shape the lives of millions, making genuine choices for many an unaffordable luxury. This is the sort of society in which women's liberation is possible, and a fundamental part of that struggle is the right to choose when or if to have children.

It's a fight we can win.

It's time for change.

Voices from the frontline

The author undertook the following interviews, which provide insightful first-hand accounts of the human consequences of attacks on women's reproductive rights. The voices represented here include women who have experienced backstreet abortion, doctors who provide reproductive health care and campaigners who have fought for a woman's right to choose. Some have already been quoted or referred to in the text; all give unique testimony to the ingenuity, courage and dedication of those on the frontline.

DR WILLIE PARKER

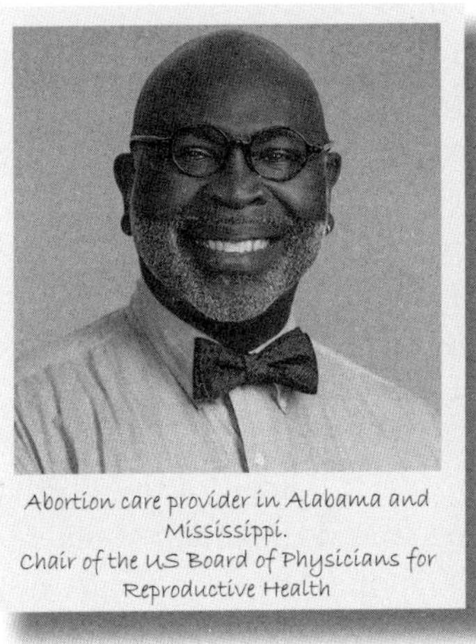

Abortion care provider in Alabama and Mississippi.
Chair of the US Board of Physicians for Reproductive Health

As a physician trained in obstetrics and gynaecology with a belief that reproductive health – as in all health – is a human right, the fact that there's an aspect of reproductive health that can be denied to a woman is a form of gender discrimination. It just doesn't square up with my values – abortion is health care. Yet there are large portions of this country where women are denied access to that care or it's made extremely difficult for them to get it. One of the regions where this is especially pronounced is the southeast region of the United States. The South, where I was born, is also the region where there are some of the highest and most intransigent levels of race and gender discrimination. I'm African American and becoming aware that 60% of all African Americans in this country live in the southeast region. The harsh laws restricting access to abortion here mean that disproportionately the women being denied access to abortion care are women of colour and poor women. Coming from that background it made it a priority for me to return to this part of the country to ensure access for women.

A woman's right to have safe and respectful care in the form of abortion should not depend on her zip code or area of residence.

So I moved back to my home town of Birmingham, and I've worked regionally by travelling to clinics throughout the southeast region where there's no provider or very few providers. That's how I ended up working in Mississippi. Mississippi has one clinic in the whole state, 55% of the population is Black and poor. So despite the fact that some people are stridently opposed to abortion – some are very vocal and some are dangerously so, you see a lot of property sabotage and very aggressive picketers who are hostile to women and providers – nevertheless the need remains. I decided that I was in a professional field that allows me to help women, where nobody else was willing to help. I started working in Mississippi in 2012, which also coincided with my decision to participate in a lawsuit to forbid the state from closing that clinic. That lawsuit is finally coming to an end and we're going to prevail and the clinic will remain open. But the political climate has shifted for the worse. We have a sitting president who has vowed to defund organisations like Planned Parenthood and appoint Supreme Court Justices who would tilt the balance of the judicial system towards overturning the Roe v Wade decision.

My compassion derives from my religious background as a Christian that says that I should provide a provide relief and assistance to people in need. And given that I'm a women's health provider the greatest need that I feel compelled to address is the fact that one in three women in this country will need an abortion by the time they are aged 45. Yet there is very limited access to these services. For the last 44 years, the overarching legal protection that women have to access abortion in this country is the decision of Roe v Wade, where the Supreme Court decided that it was a woman's right, in consultation with her doctor, to pursue the ending of a pregnancy. Individual states are allowed to make laws specific to their area but these are not allowed to supersede federal law. People opposed to abortion haven't been able to overturn the Roe decision. So there has been effort at the state level to come up with laws that, although they cannot make abortion illegal, can create so many barriers and obstacles that it can make it practically impossible for a woman to access that care.

Some examples are waiting periods. Women are required to come to the clinic, be given information (oftentimes information that is infused with misinformation) around risk associated with abortion. They have to listen to that, they have to sign a form stating that they have received that information and once they have signed that form their waiting period commences, anything from 24 to 72 hours in some states. So for women in rural areas and women with low resources or limited access to transportation this imposes a burden. They have to make round trips, sometimes three to five hours each way, to come to get the counselling, wait three days and then come back for their procedure, which often takes from five to seven minutes.

There's bans on using public funding for abortions so for example if you are poor and you have public funding for your health care, it may cover most things except for abortions. So abortion is legal, but poor woman who don't have resources have limited access. So you really have two standards of care – one for people who have means and one for people without them. There are also barriers that limit abortion based on gestational age based on junk science and the belief that a foetus can feel pain as early as six weeks. There have been bans enforced in some states so that after 20 weeks an abortion cannot be done even with a lethal foetal abnormality or when the mother's health is in jeopardy. So women who need later abortions are denied access, which can be a life-threatening situation.

These are just a few of the restrictions that hamper women's ability to access abortions. They have become somewhat ubiquitous, so they spread across parts of the country that have conservative leadership. So, for example, most of the states in the South – Alabama, Georgia, Mississippi, Louisiana, Arkansas, Texas – in total now 27 states in the US have a combination of these laws. We can say that the majority of the US is hostile to women's accessing abortion by creating barriers to them at the local level even though they cannot overturn the Roe v Wade decision.

I am clear that there are people who are ideologically driven and very strongly motivated, and some of them are moved to the point of homicide, around their perception that abortion is immoral and constitutes murder. And as a result, a number of people in this country have been killed in association with abortion care, four of them have been physicians or abortion providers. I think that anybody doing this work would be naïve to not take that into account. If they say they have no fear or concern at all I would say either they are stupid or they are being disingenuous.

So I am not stupid, nor am I disingenuous, I am aware of the risks associated with what I do. Fear is a homeostatic requirement as a safety mechanism, it's evolutionary. I jokingly say, but use it to illustrate the point, 'animals who lose their fear of their predators become lunch'. However, I believe there are two ways to approach life: you can spend your time avoiding death or you can spend your time living. I know what I live for and I'm aware that people are trying to harm me and that harm could be lethal. So I take commonsense measures and do what I can to keep myself safe. But I refuse to be cowered into not living by my deeper conviction and that is one of humanity and the equality of women. My job is to respond to the health-care needs of my patients. I'm a women's health provider. Abortion is health care. So I'm aware, I'm concerned, but I'm not deterred from doing what I know is the right thing to do.

HYUN-JU LEE

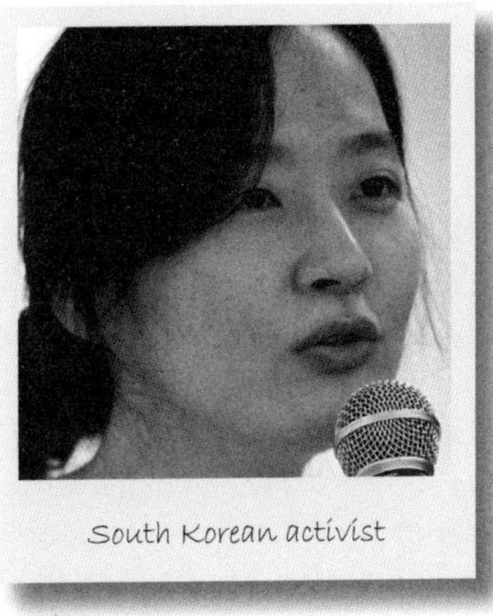

South Korean activist

The Park Geun-hye government pushed for plans to increase penalties for abortions in 2016, only to withdraw them because of strong opposition. Many women opposed the plans but the current massive movement forced the government to back down. Abortion is still illegal in Korea. It is only allowed in very rare cases and even then women must obtain the consent from her male partner. The law on abortion is out of touch with the reality. Each year hundreds of thousands of women have abortions, 95% of which fall outside the categories allowed by the existing abortion law. Women who have had an abortion are forced to keep their experiences to themselves and feel guilty. They have to pay a high cost since it is not covered by the national medical insurance. In rare cases women even get punished for abortion.

For decades, the Korean government had encouraged abortion to control birthrate. Now it talks about 'the low fertility rate crisis' and is trying to crack down on abortion. The state's attempts to control women's bodies are deeply related to the ruling class's attempts to spread conservative family values and maintain its rule on the reproduction of the workforce. In 2010, the conservative government in Korea strengthened its efforts to crack down on abortion. Many women suffered as a result. An increasing number of hospitals rejected women who needed abortions, making the cost soar to more than ten times the usual.

Many women worked in irregular jobs and could not afford the outrageous 5 million KRW [South Korean Won] for an abortion – the monthly average income of female workers in Korea is 1.62 million KRW. Women were so desperate they used the hotline run by women's groups and asked for help. Women who feared punishment travelled to other parts of the country to have an abortion under anonymity. Some even travelled to China or Japan. More and more hospitals asked for the presence of the male partner out of fear that he may report the doctor to the prosecutors later if he found out his girlfriend or wife had an abortion.

The crackdown on abortion hit poor women and teenagers unable to find the money especially hard. Even before the 2010 crackdown, a quarter of abortions on minors were performed outside hospitals or clinics because of the lack of parents' consent or money. Women must have the right to choose abortion. It was wonderful to see so many women taking to the streets against the government's plans to crack down on abortion, chanting 'my womb is mine' and asserting their 'right to choose' triumphantly.

If women do not have the right to choose abortion, they cannot control their fertility and plan their lives. Nowadays, many Korean women are participating in various social activities. But by not having the right to abortion, they can be deprived of their opportunity to receive an equal education or job, or it can be difficult to engage in political and other social activities. Even though the government has stepped back from its original plan to increase crackdowns and penalties, women will still face punishment and condemnation as long as abortion remains illegal.

ANN ROSSITER

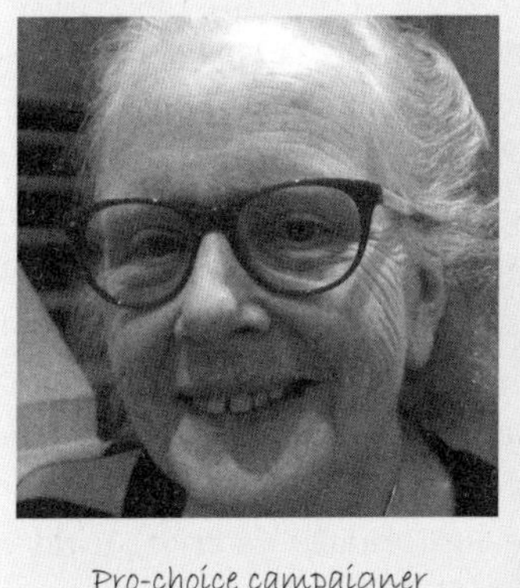

Pro-choice campaigner

To the best of my knowledge I had a backstreet abortion in 1964. I say to the best of my knowledge because for so long I put all of that to one side in my mind, because it was a very gruesome abortion, more gruesome than most. The fact that I survived was in a way miraculous. This is before the introduction of the 1967 Act. I emphasise that because I think it's important for younger people to be aware that there are people still living, quite a lot of us I imagine, who had backstreet abortions. Some indeed may have had them in Harley Street with reliable doctors, or medics, but mine was not. I've written my story and put it on YouTube and it doesn't contain all of the details. I felt that it was so difficult that people wouldn't believe me. It's funny isn't it, some things you have to hold back on because it makes it seem very unbelievable.

First of all I had no idea about anatomy when I came to England [from Ireland] or that if you engage in sexual activity, which I have to say I found very pleasant, it had consequences. I went to a Catholic boarding school until I was nearly 19 and people didn't speak about those things. The woman I went to had to repeat it three different times before it actually worked. As a result I got a perforated uterus and huge blood loss and had to be taken to St Mary's in Paddington where the medical staff were far from welcoming. It was a nuisance for them, because they had to report it to the police. I was in a fog of pain, which they didn't do much to alleviate. I was questioned and I wasn't charged but it was very traumatic. They were interested in the name of the abortionist. She had presented herself as a seamstress, in those days loads of alterations of clothes went on. She had very little expertise, and certainly she was doing it for the money. It was a very frightening experience, and that's what started me on track arguing that, if women were going to have an abortion it should be safe and legal.

When you get something that traumatic either you shut down or you do the opposite, which is become a campaigner, which is what happened to me. The nurses' night-to-day duty changeover happened around 8am and the sister of a girl I was at school with came on duty. I had to endure a very large mouthful from her. As a result of which, and the attitude of the doctors, I discharged myself on the spot. It was a very dangerous thing to do because I was suffering from all sorts of damage and I know I had a severe infection, but I was young and I was strong.

Then I went to live in Spain, under Franco if you were caught it was not quite a capital offence but not far off it. I discovered there were two Spains – aboveground and belowground, unlike Ireland where it was all pretty and strict overground and underground. That was my introduction to all of it. When I came back to England I got involved with the National Abortion Campaign (NAC). But in the midst of all of the pro-choice activities I became aware that of course they didn't even have contraception in the Republic of Ireland. It seemed incongruous that I was spending an enormous amount of my spare time working on reproductive rights here, and nothing for there. So that's what set me off on working on issues to do with Ireland and I've been involved since.

I was in the Irish Women's Abortion Support Group for the 20 years of its existence, most of the time I worked putting women up [who came to Britain for abortions] and I still do.

We were all active in the British feminist movement and it was an organic thing, somebody would ring me and ask me to find out about clinics. We didn't have any network, just throughout the year there would be quite a number of guests for dinner on a Friday night. They would stay until Sunday evening, and would disappear for at least one night. The NHS was quite strict on that, because of safety interests. They would worry that women would go back to Ireland and if they had bleeding or any of those situations that they wouldn't go to a GP. So this began to become an organisation. But always voluntary, many of us had full-time jobs, families and children. Spare time would be spent filling forms and jumping through the cracks in bureaucracy.

We always raised money ourselves and we had enormous fun as well as it being fairly grim, because in a way we created an alternative Irish community. We'd put on cèilidhs, and nobody had ever heard of a lesbian cèilidh before. Nor would they ever imagine that one of the most traditional and possible most reactionary forces, the cèilidh, would be transformed into a joyous affair of celebration. There was a lot of fun involved, anyone who thinks that those years were all just grim, they weren't. We worried dreadfully for the women who came, who were ringing us from telephone boxes in the rural areas. If you were ringing from Belfast to London it was considered a local call, whereas if you were ringing from Dublin to here it was an international call and it had to go through an operator. Local operators snooped in on people's calls and quite a number of women were exposed through that. So we then devised this codeword for an abortion, because the restrictions were so severe from the mid-1980s on any kind of information. We decided to call an abortion 'Imelda', a good Irish-Catholic name, to try and fox the telephone operators who would snitch on you in a local area where everyone knew everybody, and more about you than you knew about yourself.

Now I'm not involved in the day-to-day arrangements, Mara Clarke in the Abortion Support Network does all of that. But I do work with 'Speaking of Imelda' [a feminist performance group], which I find incredibly empowering, because the power of the visual representation is tremendous. I have learnt a great deal. I did stand-up for a while, 'Making a Holy Show of Yourself', and everybody in those days said, oh my God, this is disgusting you can't make fun of abortions and people seeking abortions, and sure I believe all that, but at least let's look at the silences involved and that is, if not funny, it's very ironic.

EMMA CAMPBELL

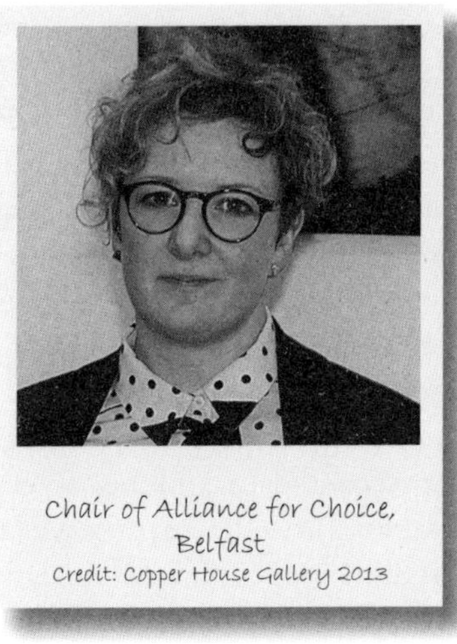

Chair of Alliance for Choice, Belfast
Credit: Copper House Gallery 2013

We have been campaigning from probably 2000, originally for the extension of the 1967 Act but now we campaign for the full decriminalisation. We believe that the abortion pills and the accessibility of telemedicine have changed the needs of the legal framework. We think that the issue has forced our government into a bit of a tight corner because they can't just extend the 1967 Act either – not that they've ever wanted to. In the last five years the public conversation has really changed. Before it was just a very black-and-white issue. It was 'yes' or 'no' and there was so much stigma and secrecy about abortion that nobody wanted to share their story. Nobody wanted to be the one to put their hand up and say 'I've had an abortion' and that's obviously changing – slightly. I think there's an influence from the Campaign to Repeal the Eighth in the South, from the Abortion Rights Campaign and others.

We've had people from the north talking about their experience of buying pills and we've had a lot of women speaking to journalists anonymously about their own experience of having an abortion. It is has taken back the conversation from lawmakers, politicians and religious leaders. It's given voice to the people for whom it matters the most – the people who need to have abortions. As an activist it's heartening and disheartening because we can see the public mood is really changing. We feel that 90% of people would describe themselves as pro-choice, even if they wouldn't have an abortion themselves. Unfortunately, the Assembly doesn't match that public opinion. Part of the reason for that, I think especially in Northern Ireland, is because quite a large proportion of the population still vote along community lines. They aren't voting on social issues. Now this is changing. In the North Belfast constituency there were five pro-choice candidates. This has never happened before. The most we ever had openly pro-choice people in the Assembly was two. But actually there are new, younger voices coming through – the Green Party has two candidates and they are a pro-choice party. People Before Profit is a pro-choice party. We know from private conversations that there are people who are definitely pro-choice in the larger parties but there's a huge whip and they can't do anything about it. With the marriage equality Bill in the South and the famous Ashers cake scandal about a bakery not wanting to bake a cake for gay marriage rights – all that brought issues of rights and human bodily integrity and autonomy more into the conversation and public discourse in Northern Ireland. And people are being asked on the doorstep about abortion and gay rights.

We don't believe that the law in Northern Ireland stops abortions, it just drives them underground and makes them happen later and makes them more expensive and more traumatic. And the stigma from it being illegal actually creates more mental health problems than any from actually having an abortion. So that's why now it's both heartening and disheartening at the same time.

SINÉAD KENNEDY

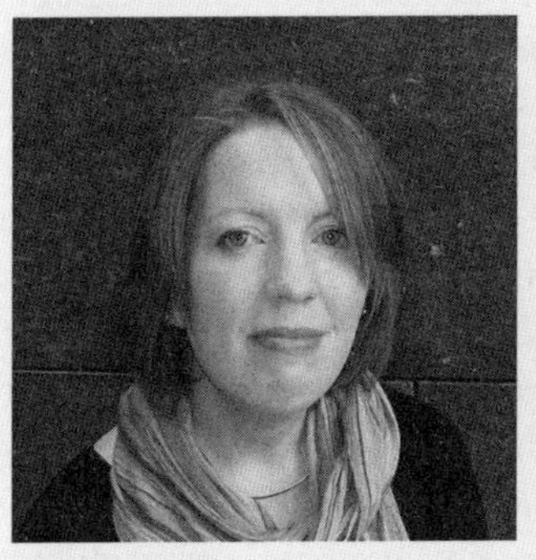

Secretary of The Coalition to Repeal the Eighth Amendment

Things have dramatically changed in Ireland since 2012 and the death of Savita Halappanavar. It had been tipping for a very long time. Ireland was forever up in front of the European Courts of Human Rights and Justice being sanctioned and told it had to do something. The government would nod and say: 'Oh but what can we do' and would try to kick it down the line and nothing would happen. The day after the story broke a small protest had been scheduled and thousands of people turned up. Then another one was called for the Saturday and again just thousands and thousands of people turned up in a way that you just don't see in Dublin. The government was forced into action. Then you see what has happened over the last couple of years.

There is this explosion of anger and it's mainly among young women. I'd say 15 to 25 year olds are 85% of the abortion movement in Ireland. It's exploding in all sorts of creative and interesting ways. Every time you go on social media you find a new group as sprung up and all sorts of protests and creative actions are being organised. People go around nightclubs and put stickers on bathroom doors saying this is where you need to go if you want information on how to get an abortion and this is what to do to access the abortion pill. It's everywhere. A lot of it is just a couple of people getting together and saying 'let's do this, let's organise around that'. That is what is kind of fantastic about it and that is also what's putting an awful lot of pressure on the government. They don't quite know how to respond. So there's all of this anger, all this spontaneous action and of course there are the official campaigning groups. The umbrella organisation, The Coalition to Repeal the Eighth Amendment, has 70 different organisations around the country and collectively it represents about a million and a half people. So that is pretty important.

The reality for Irish women has been that if you could scramble the money together you could go to Britain. We know that at least 150,000 women have accessed an abortion in Britain and this has contained the situation a little bit. You don't see backstreet abortions in Ireland in the way you might see in other countries where abortion is not accessible through a neighboring state. The question of class is always central to this because it's about who gets access to abortion. Sometimes activists get caught up in the perfect law or legislation, but at the end of the day it's very much about access. That is why the abortion pill has been a complete game changer in some ways, although again not everyone can access it.

The referendum on equal marriage was also a game changer in Irish society. People want to think they are open and compassionate and will support women and some think a new referendum on abortion will be like the equal marriage vote. But the issue of abortion in Irish society is so divisive and so entrenched. I think there will be a referendum and I think we will win it, but it will be a battle. The equal marriage campaign was won on love, marriage, families and smiling babies. You can't do that on abortion – it will be more hard fought. For example, anti-choicers have accused pro-choice people of wanting to eradicate Down's syndrome. Yet the very same politicians stood up and voted for devastating cuts to community services, sometimes including for people with special needs. Ireland is not like Britain, there is no NHS and contraception is still very expensive. Going to your doctor costs between 50 and 70 euro a visit. So even basic contraceptive care is difficult to obtain in Ireland.

People also look at the contradictions. There is a constitutional prohibition on abortion in Ireland but also a constitutional right to travel to have an abortion. It's like the government is saying, 'we don't care, go off to England, take your pills, have an abortion. Just don't have them in Ireland, don't talk about it'. They want to live in the facade of being a 'pro-life' country, which values the unborn. All this is feeding into debates about what type of society we live in. People are asking how are women going to care for all these children they're being forced to have. It's fundamental to the nature of capitalist society and the era of neoliberal capitalism. Governments are attacking the very things women need to care for children.

There are tactical and strategic questions about how to win a referendum. I hope it will simply ask do you want to remove this from the Irish constitution or do you want to keep it? But there is debate about what does the movement ask for, do we go out and ask for choice and make the argument for choice? I think we have to very openly argue for that. But already some more conservative parts of the movement are saying, 'we don't want scare people off.' There is pressure to look respectable and not to be too 'shrill' or too angry. Abortion on demand is the spectre used. Some argue that we can go for abortion in cases of rape, incest and fatal foetal abnormality and maybe even for reasons of health, but not on demand or on request. So there are tensions about what we ask for and that will be one of the big challenges for the movement.

Young women want to argue for choice. They reject an incremental view and the opinion polls show 45–55% of people support choice, which is pretty great given that you rarely hear that argument rehearsed in the media or elsewhere. It shows there is a lot of space and scope to make those arguments.

DENISE

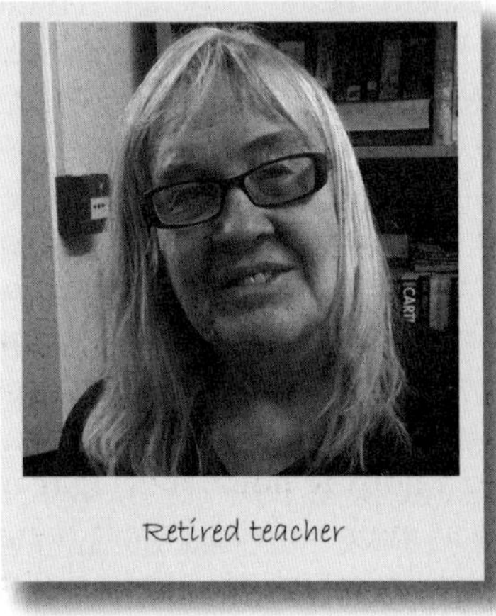

Retired teacher

I got pregnant when I was about 23, and this was at a time when having illegitimate children was still viewed in a very hostile way. I remember a lot of the attitudes that were around then and when I was a teenager. For example, one of the worst things you could say about another girl was that she had lost her reputation. Which is a very strange thing to say, we think today. But everyone said it in those days and that actually meant that she had slept with her boyfriend, or she'd had sex in some way, and people had found out.

I became a teacher and had been to college but I became pregnant with my regular boyfriend. But I thought at that time that I couldn't have a baby. I didn't really want to have a baby. I certainly couldn't tell my parents. My parents would have been horrified that I, as an unmarried woman, had done something as awful as have sex with my boyfriend. Those were the days when life was very different from what it is today and I decided I had to have an abortion. I had to get my teacher career up and running, that's what I wanted to do. So I had to find a way of finding a doctor who was prepared to do the abortion. I didn't want to do a backstreet abortion. I knew that they existed. But I wanted to have an abortion that was done by a qualified person, which I knew was going to cost money.

So in fact I was able through a friend to find the name of a surgeon who was prepared to do it, and then I had to find the money, which I think at the time was £60. This doesn't sound a lot now but in those days it was rather something. In fact I borrowed that money from my parents. I told them that it was down payment or the security for a flat. A big lie but I got the money and I went to see the doctor. I kind of knew what sort of things you had to say. I told the doctor that I couldn't possibly have this baby, it was making me very depressed and if I had to have the baby I would commit suicide. I think that was more or less standard practice. It enabled the doctor to say, 'oh well, from the point of view of your personal health and safety' he would do that abortion.

So I went into a nursing home overnight and the operation took place with no problem and I went home. I certainly did not in any way get depressed about it. I was quite happy about it. It seemed to me to be perfectly all right. So since then I have always told people that I had an abortion. It had no contrary effects on me – it was a good thing to do. If people were talking to me about whether it was a good thing to have an abortion I would say if it suits you, you should. It's much better to do that than to bring a child into the world who is unwanted and unloved. Any child that we have has got to be a wanted child. So that was my abortion experience.

DIANE MUNDAY

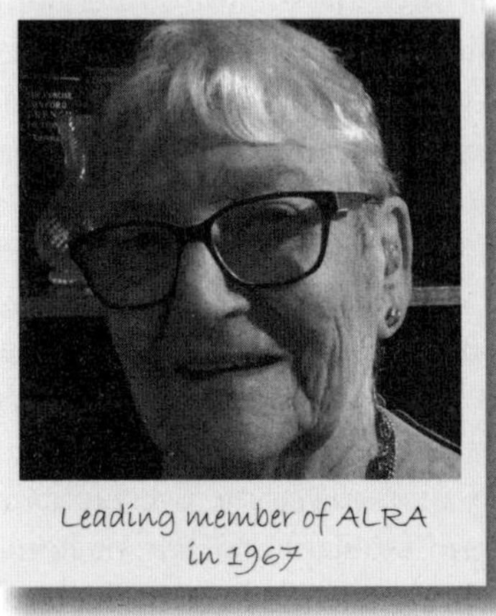

Leading member of ALRA in 1967

Back in the 1960s 'abortion' was a word that was never ever used. Later, I came to discover that virtually every woman had some kind of experience of it, either for herself or for her family. For example, one of the very first meetings I spoke at was the afternoon branch of a Townswomen's Guild. These tended to be older ladies because young mums went to the evening ones. There were all these very respectable-looking ladies wearing hats and gloves and I started off by saying, 'I have had an abortion'. I was always upfront about it. I used my own experience. But I was absolutely staggered because it was the first time I had an experience, which later became quite commonplace. During the tea break when they brought homemade cakes and plates with doilies on, and dainty cups and saucers, they came up to me one after another. They each said something like, 'I had an abortion, dear, I never told anybody', or 'my sister had an abortion', 'I looked after a friend', 'because it was the Depression and my husband was out of work, I've never told anybody before'. I came to realise that this was deep in the consciousness of most women but it was something that they never spoke about.

So when I became pregnant with an unwanted pregnancy, it was my fourth in four years – these were before the days of the pill and things – I just knew I couldn't face coping with another child. Because I had a chequebook to wave in Harley Street I bought myself a safe abortion. It cost a great deal of money. It was £90, which in those days was a huge amount. We had no holiday that year and we cut back on everything. But coming round from the anaesthetic I suddenly remembered something that I must have pushed into my subconscious. When I first started work I had a friend who was a dressmaker in east London. In those days there were lots of dressmakers as people had their clothes made. She had three young children, a husband that worked in a local factory and she was making a dress for me. One day when I got in from work and was going around there to have a fitting my mother said to me, 'I've got some very bad news for you. She's dead'. It transpired that she had had a backstreet abortion. And of course she was much in the situation that I later found myself in with three very young children. Perhaps her inability to cope was even greater than mine. They lived in a prefabricated hut, which was used for housing after the war. She wasn't a bad mother, in fact it was because she was a good mother that she felt that she couldn't have another child.

I suddenly realised the inequality and the unfairness of the fact that because we were able to raise the money, I was alive. My children had a mother and my husband had a wife. Because she couldn't raise that sort of money, she was dead. I made some sort of anaesthetic-muddled vow to myself. I would spend the rest of my life fighting for other women to have what I saw then, and still see, as the privilege of the ability to terminate a pregnancy safely, when it was at the wrong time and the wrong place in the wrong circumstances. That was how I got involved. It was just about the time of the thalidomide stories and there was a letter in one of the Sunday newspapers mentioning the Abortion Law Reform Association. As a result of that I joined, as did a lot of people. I went along to a meeting of the almost-defunct, moribund Abortion Law Reform Association that the older generation had kept going throughout the war. Indeed there had been one Bill in parliament – Kenneth Robinson's Bill at the beginning of the 1960s, which was defeated. Having never been involved in anything at all within a year I found myself on the committee and elected as the Vice Chairman. From then on, apart from a husband and three children, it dominated right through until 1967 when I carried on fighting to keep it legal. Then as one of the founder members of the British Pregnancy Advisory Service, I just kept fighting.

JANE MCKAY

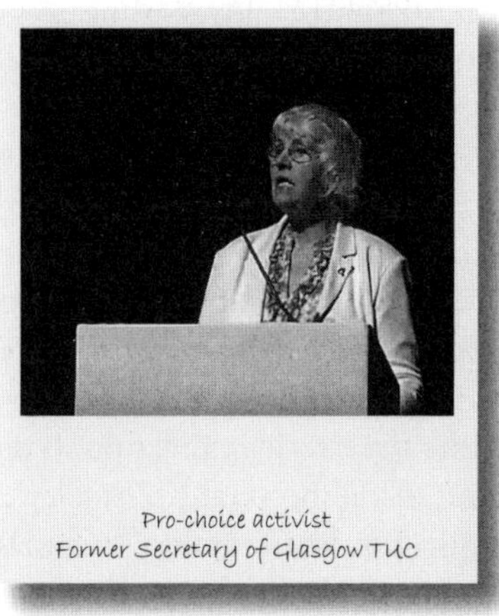

Pro-choice activist
Former Secretary of Glasgow TUC

I was always supportive of a woman's right to choose, I didn't quite realise I would be faced with the problem myself. The Abortion Act came into being in 1967 and I think most people/ women would have thought great this has opened the door to stop backstreet abortions. But unfortunately it didn't quite work that way for many women. I was probably in retrospect one of the fortunate ones. It was the early 1970s and I had two youngsters of my own and then became pregnant because of the failure of the cap. I went to my doctor who was very good and sympathetic and he referred me to the local hospital.

I went to see a doctor there and I was quite appalled and upset when I was given an examination similar to what one would expect when in late stages of pregnancy and what upset me was the doctor saying 'now now mummy', which drove me up the wall. I got angry and upset and said I wasn't here for the continuation of a pregnancy, I was here for a termination. I duly jumped off the medical couch got dressed and left the hospital. Prior to that he advised me that I would have to go and see a psychiatrist after seeing him. I said I wasn't in any way mentally disturbed before I came here, that I had a medical problem but by the time they had finished with me I would. So I left the hospital.

I ended up at my doctor's again and by this time the anger had spilled to tears. He took me into the surgery and I explained what had happened. He then lifted the phone and contacted another hospital, it was the only women's hospital we had in Glasgow, which is no longer there. I went to see another doctor within a matter of days and got a termination.

However there were aspects that I found quite stressful. Namely some of the staff and their attitude towards women, which I hope is not happening in today's world. They were not kind and considerate towards you. Many women including myself were in absolute pain after the termination but really didn't receive the appropriate medication. I was fortunate because the Sister of the ward on one of the evenings happened to be a relative of mine and she gave me the necessary medication to deal with the pain.

After I came out of the hospital I sent a letter to the hospital explaining my concerns. But I couldn't tell many people. There were very few people who were aware at that time I had a termination. It wasn't until quite a few years after that I was able to speak about it. This was because of the pressure on women at that time. When I think of what women went through at that time I would never like to see that done again. It horrifies me to think that there are continuous attacks on the Abortion Act. Women don't go into a termination in a frivolous manner. It is something they have thought about and in some cases talked through with their partner. It is not taken upon lightly. I go back to the old arguments – it is a women's right to choose. I hope that young women today will recognise that and continue to monitor what's happening to women in the situation I was in.

ANNE KANE

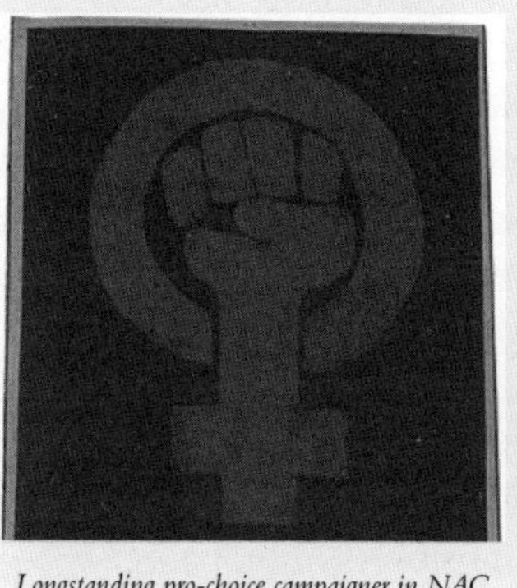

Longstanding pro-choice campaigner in NAC and Abortion Rights

Disabled people's rights are being undermined on a whole series of fronts, directly and indirectly. These attacks are threatening gains made over decades by disabled people themselves. Legal rights often go unenforced, discrimination in employment and education remains rife, attacks on welfare provision represent life-and-death threats to many disabled people and are certainly an attack on dignity. All this threatens the status of disabled people in society increasing prejudice and stigma. This is part of the context in which discussions on abortion law take place.

Current abortion law is imperfect in a number of ways. Doctors, not women, have the right to decide and abortion remains subject to the criminal law. The law has been shaped by the medical establishment and wider political opinion, as well as by longstanding pressure from women or the feminist movement. There was a eugenicist element in the history of the abortion law reform movement, one which the feminist movement challenged and changed as part of the movement for choice. This included raising the profile and rights of disabled women themselves –

challenging assumptions such as that disabled women couldn't be good mothers, shouldn't reproduce, didn't have a sexuality in fact. I'm aware of this history as a feminist and as a disabled person.

The provision in the law for termination on grounds of foetal abnormality is broad and subject to interpretation. And of course, termination, under any of the grounds of the law, is always a decision taken by women in their real conditions of life. The choices we make in this sense are always subject to pressure.

Nevertheless, I find it impossible to see the benefit of any position other than one whereby women's rights to make a choice and not to be forced to continue a termination are respected. Restricting abortion rights would not improve the position of disabled people. That requires action to defend the rights and living conditions of disabled people as such, of people here and now. Respecting women's rights (including disabled women's rights) to choose whether or not to continue or to terminate a pregnancy – for any reason covered by the law – is the only possible position.

At the same time, choice has to be as real as possible. That means limiting pressures from the medical establishment, public or political opinion or as a result of a lack of rights or material support. An assumption that a particular course should be taken if a test produces a particular result, or if the woman is in a particular social situation, is directive and not about choice. No woman should be forced either to terminate or carry on with a pregnancy. Women should have the time and support to make their own choices.

YVONNE WILKIN

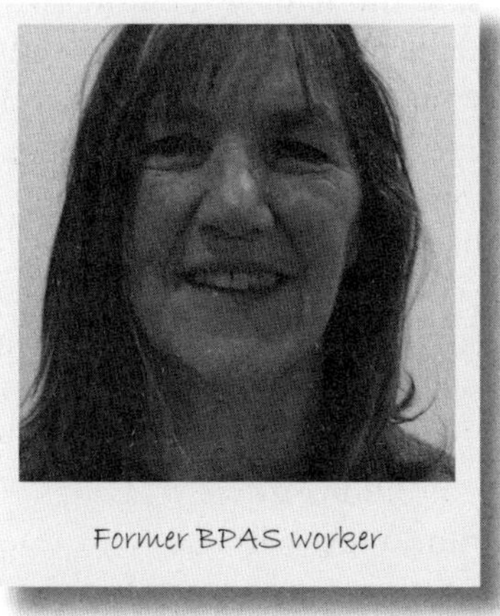

Former BPAS worker

I worked at the British Pregnancy Advisory Service in London Victoria during the 1970s, which was a new branch at the time of a national organisation. I was part of the counselling team within the branch. So I had direct experience face to face with women both in the counselling situation and also when women rang up. At that time we still needed to be very clear with women about the legal situation and how we'd help them sympathetically but in the context of a political framework. We had to be aware that, because there were organisations and individuals that would have liked to pull our services down, you could have someone on the phone who was only pretending to be a woman enquiring. It could easily have been an anti-choice person, or even a member of the press pretending to be a woman and looking for an angle to have a go at abortion services. So we were always very, very particular to explain what a consultation would entail, that there would be sympathetic doctors with a legal framework, two doctors and they would be deciding whether or not to approve the abortion and under what grounds.

I've done various other kinds of work. I've been a computer programmer and a social worker and other things. But for me now that I'm retired and I look back at those years – it was such a constructive time! Obviously I was also involved in pro-choice marches, and all that kind of thing. There was a huge amount of emotion on a day-to-day basis working with women in that kind of struggle and sometimes their partners, their sisters who came along with them. If they came in and then wanted to changed their minds that was obviously okay also, because we were about being pro-choice, not pro-abortion. So it means a heck of a lot to me.

JAN NIELSEN

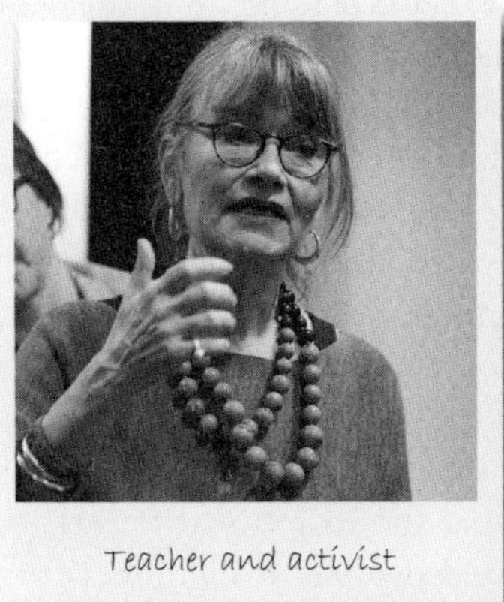

Teacher and activist

The campaign against the Corrie Bill in 1979 was really exciting. Within the National Abortion Campaign [NAC] we could see we were winning individual trade-union branches to the argument that abortion wasn't just an issue for women. We argued that it wasn't a personal issue but it was a political one that trade unionists needed to be involved in. I was aware that there were people like myself, particularly women, in various union branches who had lost the argument in previous years. But around Corrie the argument started to be won and you could see the union branches going down, like dominoes really.

Once one union branch had adopted it, which I believe was initially the NUT [National Union of Teachers], it was then much easier to win it in other trade-union branches. My experience was in East London and I can remember two workplaces in particular. One was the Ford's Dagenham car plant where we knew a few socialist men who worked there. We produced a regular socialist bulletin for Ford workers. I met (myself and another woman) with a group of socialists above a cafe where the men used to go after the morning shift. On several Friday mornings we had discussions about what arguments had come up in the Ford's branch and how they could handle them. It's important to remember that at the time the women workers at Ford's Dagenham were in a completely separate machine shop and union branch. So there was a lot of preparation and discussion about how best to put those pro-choice arguments in bulletins in the weeks leading up to the demonstration called by the TUC in October 1979.

The other workplace was actually in the social security offices in Stratford and around East London where again different people we met took up the arguments. Of course when Ford's Dagenham passed the motion in support of defending abortion rights it was a fantastic feeling. It was a massive step forward to see it passed at an all-male trade union branch.

On the day of the TUC march itself it was, how can I say, it was a very, very different feel to other demonstrations. Firstly, my memory is that the march was at least 40% men. We had always had the odd dribble of men, socialist men, supporting NAC, but to have men carrying all your very traditional trade union banners on that demonstration – we knew that we had crossed the Rubicon. We knew that we had gone into a totally different political period and I can't tell you how elated we all felt to see Len Murray leading the demonstration. We didn't have any illusions about him but that was such an important step to have the TUC general secretary leading a demonstration to defend abortion rights.

Although we didn't win lots of the demands around access to abortion that we wanted, the power of the unity of men and women across working-class organisations and the trade unions meant that other anti-abortion figures did not come back in a hurry. They didn't follow Corrie with the rapidity that they might have done. If it hadn't been for the trade union movement taking it on, and the protest we achieved, they might have whacked us over Corrie and we would have had more bigots coming forward immediately afterwards.

MARIA FYFE

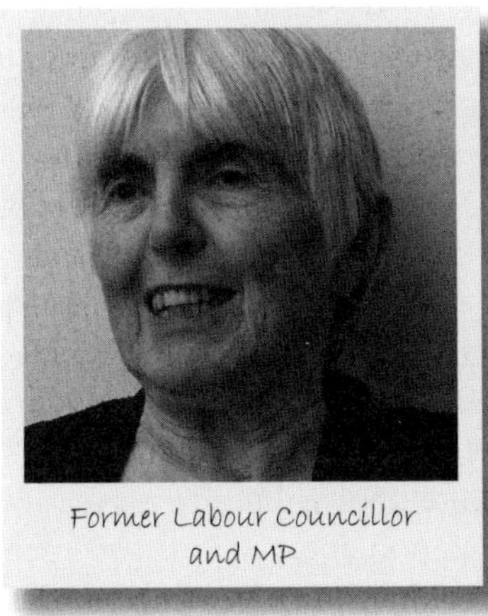

Former Labour Councillor and MP

My own beginning to think about abortion as a human right goes back long before I was either a councillor or an MP. I was brought up a Catholic and taught to think that abortion was wrong in all circumstances. I was a young married woman in my mid-20s living in a housing scheme in Glasgow known as Drumchapel. I had a baby son and an infant son. A friend of mine came knocking at my door one day, urgently. She was on her way home from an illegal abortion, which was in 1966 before the Abortion Act. She was bleeding heavily. I got her to my flat and I was really worried about how heavily she was bleeding. I said to her: 'You can't go on like that; you could end up dying, I need to get a doctor'. In fact the bleeding did stop shortly after that but I thought it was safer to bring her down the road to see my doctor. He confirmed that she was safe to go home and he did nothing to report it. I knew he wouldn't, he was a decent guy.

My friend was in desperate straits because she couldn't have a legal abortion and that made me think more closely about these matters. Many years later when I was in parliament, it must have been in 1987, I hadn't been thinking particularly about abortion issues but they arose because of the Alton Bill [a Bill to cut abortion time limits; see Chapter Five].

Sometime shortly after I was elected, Jo Richardson MP, who was a doughty fighter for women and a stalwart supporter of abortion rights, made me her deputy, which I was delighted to do. She was a total example, a real flag waver for us all. Anyway, the Alton Bill came about and when it comes to an issue of conscience, which is how abortion is seen, members of parliament have a free vote. The whips don't help, they stand back from it all. Neither Jo or I had any experience whatsoever of whipping but we got some excellent people to our side. Tony Banks MP was excellent. I'll never forget the way he stood outside the doors to the voting lobbies when the vote was taking place. Instead of just saying support amendment three or whatever, go this way or that, he was saying: 'Pope and Paisley that side! Women for choice this side!'. It was great because there were many clauses and amendments and members who'd not been sitting in the chamber – they had other things to do such as sitting on committees – if they were on our side they wanted to be clear which door to enter to vote.

We managed to defeat the Alton Bill. There'd been a big march and rally in Glasgow and I have kept a much-treasured photograph of that occasion where Jo is addressing a huge crowd in a public hall in Glasgow and I'm chairing the meeting. Jo and I marched at the front of this big march through Glasgow defending abortion rights. That's just a great memory for me. We faced terrible opposition. I found very mixed messages coming from my constituents. Two of the parish priests were absolutely shocked that I was doing this because I think they assumed that I must be a Catholic because of my name. My full name was O'Neill because I'd changed my name to Fyfe in marriage as you did in those days. One of them invited me to come and defend my actions to the Women's Guild, which I said I'd be glad to do so. I said I'd also like to tell them about the pro-life actions that I do take on, like supporting international aid and projects to help women get an education and so forth. The invitation never came after that!

But I also got amazing support from women in the street who'd stop me to thank me. I was just amazed at that. They were just so hugely relieved that the Alton Bill had been defeated. Now and again we still have to defend abortion rights and from time to time there were other battles in parliament but none were as exciting and interesting as that that. So since retiring from parliament I decided to be involved in the Scottish Abortion Rights campaign.

DR JAYNE KAVANAGH

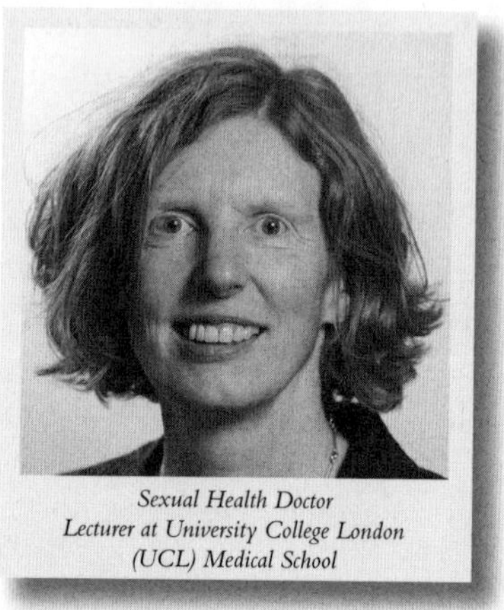

Sexual Health Doctor
Lecturer at University College London (UCL) Medical School

I'm a sexual health doctor, I work at a contraceptive clinic part time and I'm also responsible for teaching abortion to medical students at UCL Medical School.

It's only been in the last few years that I've started to talk to students about questioning the current law, about the possibility of decriminalisation, in terms of clinical benefit – of not having a law that interferes in clinical good practice – and also in terms of respecting women's autonomy and reducing the stigma that plagues abortion.

That's come on the back of the 2012 so-called *Telegraph* sex-selection stings, where there was a threat of prosecution for two doctors accused of authorising unlawful abortions. They weren't prosecuted in the end, but I think there was a lot of anxiety after that. Coupled with the fact that shortly afterwards the Care Quality Commission visited many abortion clinics throughout the country specifically looking for pre-signed HSA1 [abortion] forms. They found a handful of doctors who had pre-signed abortion forms and left them in clinics with Clause C ringed, which allows abortion to be carried out if the threat to the physical or mental health of the woman is greater than if the pregnancy continued.

I know some of the doctors who were reported to the General Medical Council [GMC] for this, and they are very competent, committed clinicians, who had done this because they thought it was the best way to run their clinics. In many abortion clinics now women are seen by nurses, very competent and professional nurses. So doctors had pre-signed the abortion form to speed the process up for women for good clinical reasons – because two doctors' signatures are needed to authorise an abortion. They knew and trusted the nurses, they understood the governance procedures in their clinics, and also they felt they could justify it legally, which is right, because an abortion under 24 weeks is safer than a pregnancy proceeding to term.

Even though their actions could be legally justified they were reported to the GMC. Before this, we thought that the law was working in favour of women, allowing doctors and nurses to get on and give women the abortions they chose to have. But it was at that point that I began to seriously consider the potential impact of having a law governing abortion, of the risk of doctors and women being prosecuted and actually going to prison.

I think we had become complacent because there hadn't been any of this kind of activity for years. So that really hit home with me and a lot of other doctors, and for other reasons as well, which I'll come to, that we'd be far better off if there wasn't a law on abortion, and it was just regulated like all other medical procedures.

After this I started to talk to health-care professionals and medical students about the possibility of decriminalising abortion, mostly in terms of clinical good practice. For example, nurses can't prescribe the medical abortion pills, which they can if the woman has had a miscarriage. So they're prescribing the same medication in one clinical situation but not another and it's preventing committed, competent health-care professionals from working fully in abortion care. Women also have to come back to the abortion clinic for the second abortion pill, where there's a risk of them starting to bleed on the way home, rather than giving them two pills on the same visit, which decriminalisation would allow for.

Also, doctors and nurses, instead of focusing on the interests of the woman in front of them, could be thinking: 'What do I need to document in order to justify this abortion?' Plus two doctors having to authorise the abortion, and all the implications for women's autonomy, and the stigma associated with something being a criminal offence.

So all of those things have led me to believe, over the course of the last few years, that decriminalising abortion is important for clinical and social progress. So I've started flagging up the issue whenever appropriate, of the implications of abortion falling under a statute like the Offences Against the Person Act 1861 for good clinical practice, respect for women's autonomy and tackling stigma.

So that's where I am at with my professional work in terms of medical education and campaigning, I am 100% behind the move to decriminalise abortion. When I'm in clinic speaking to women who need an abortion, I don't want to be thinking at the back of my mind: 'What are the possible legal ramifications, for me and for this woman in this particular context?' I want to be focused on doing what's best for the woman in front of me. That's one of the many reasons I support the move to decriminalise abortion.

DR KATE GUTHRIE

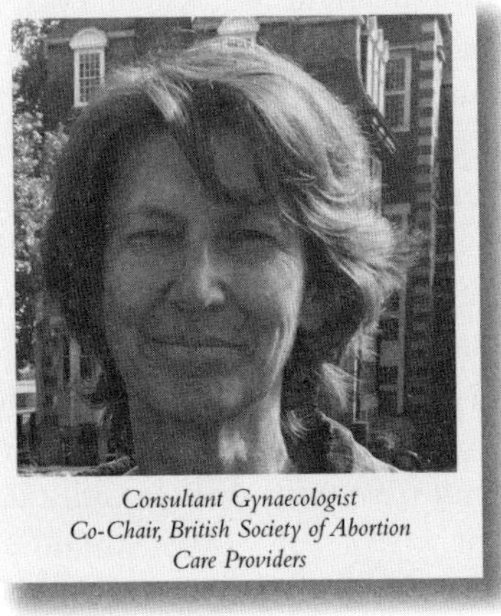

Consultant Gynaecologist
Co-Chair, British Society of Abortion Care Providers

If you are in work and have already got dependent children and you have to get two buses to a clinic, finance can be a real disabler. Women in low-paid jobs sometimes miss appointments. But for women who are insistent to end the pregnancy one of the drivers not to continue is finance, particularly if they've got children already. One of the really tough decisions is: 'I have children. I want to give them the best I have. I want to give them the best start in life maybe unlike my own start in life … And if another child comes along then I'm depriving my existing children and making this difficult decision about deciding whether to have another child.'

So abortion provision has to be something that is more accessible. Then you've got confidentiality and that's part of that stigma – either the real or perceived stigma women have to go through. Access to some services might be through the general reception desk, which could be in a general practice, a general hospital or outpatient clinic. You can guarantee committed abortion providers will not be judgemental. But women sometimes have to go through people whose job it is to answer the phone or to meet and greet, who don't sign up to choice and can give women a hard time. Or women may just perceive they are being given a hard time, or maybe they had an abortion before and been told: 'I don't want to see you back here again'. So they anticipate a hard time.

I suspect an increasing number of women are going online. There's information from the States saying that women are going online and saying: 'I already bought stuff and none of it works'. But that's because it wasn't an abortion pill, it was chalk! Some of the American providers check every new company that crops up on the internet, they order pills and test the chems in the pills. But for the women who are desperate, a) they are still pregnant and b) they are even more pregnant than they were before so their options are reduced.

So looking to abortion provision in the future, the actual clinical provision of care, it has to be something that destigmatises. Women should not have to run the gauntlet at multiple levels – financial and social – to access care. Right now you can turn up for a scan but then you have to come to the providers twice for two sorts of pills for an early abortion. Which is what women are increasingly demanding – they know they are pregnant at an early stage. They are very clear that they never wanted this pregnancy, and they want it over and done with as quickly as possible. So it's about building a future service for women based upon what women want and what women's needs are, which doesn't have them hiking around the country with their cap in their hand. Because if we can get women-led type of service then it's actually incredibly cheap, successful, functional and safe.

So my vision – women are happy to access contraception and emergency contraception online. So if it's something straightforward then do it online. This requires a change in the law. For more complex stuff you'd have to see a health-care provider. We should be respecting and supplying what women need. I want to see more of use of the internet/telephone and less clinic visits and I support getting rid of all the other 'inconveniences' of the current law which are not necessary today: criminalisation, two signatures, doctors only for surgical procedures, not having to swallow pills in licensed premises.

There's a lot of lessons to be learnt about how we could give much more appropriate services that are currently held back by regulation at multiple levels.

DR TRACEY MASTERS

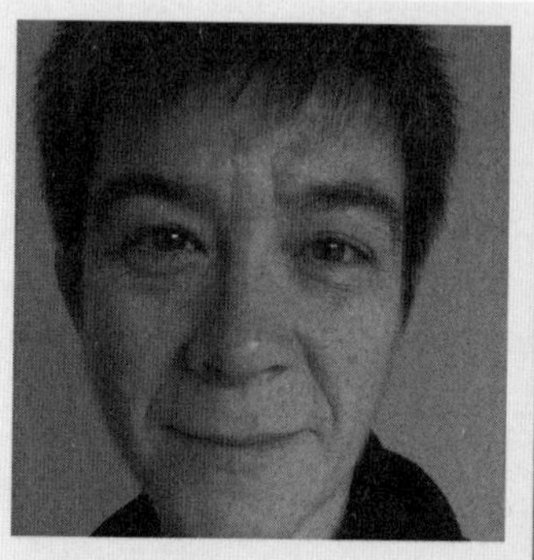

Consultant in Sexual and Reproductive Health
Abortion care provider

You asked me to say something about what abortion might look like in the future if we took away all the restrictions and dealt with much of the stigma that shapes what happens now. It's nice to be able to fantasise about these things. I would have this idea that, rather than women having to make an immediate decision at the time of their pregnancy being first diagnosed – to choose to go and see a midwife and book their antenatal care, or choose to go and talk to someone in an abortion care service – that we actually didn't make a distinction. Instead we gave people a pathway that starts off without any kind of pre-defined ideas. This is because otherwise you inherently bring in an element of stigma that is inappropriate.

Of course, lots of people do know pretty much the minute they do their pregnancy test which way they are going to go. But there are an awful lot of women that don't. Making life easy for them and giving them a comfortable space in which they can explore all the different avenues would be my idea of a significantly different way forward. So if somebody came along and they happened to find that their pregnancy wasn't viable, they would have a miscarriage and wouldn't have to see a different group of people. That's happening a little bit now in quite a few services. But I think extrapolating from that to a wider sort of pregnancy care, that's my vision for the future.

It is easy for people who don't work in abortion care, and that includes health professionals and the general public, to not appreciate how much of an impact the law has. We try to work round it so that the women themselves don't feel and see it. But you realise when you start to analyse things just how much it does impact. You create these different pathways and once you have done that you start to develop groups of people who work too independently from each other. Services are currently either one or the other, either about continuing pregnancies or about where abortion has been chosen.

In England and Wales abortion care has been seen as somehow different from other forms of health care. Such a lot of it has been provided by independent providers, you then get this division. So people dealing with other women's health issues nowadays very rarely get exposure to abortion care. So it is kind of 'exceptionalising' of abortion and this legal stuff exacerbates that. It is increasingly proving dangerous because we no longer have the workforce building up skills to provide and actually understand [abortion].

It's a vicious cycle as the more it becomes separated off from ordinary health care the less that people understand it and the more the stigma around it happens. So many people, even those who work with in health care and even people who work within women's health care, will be surprised at how common abortion is – when you tell them that at least one in three women have an abortion by the time they get to 30. They don't see abortion nowadays because it is separated. I think this has been a massive mistake. I'm hopeful we can work towards changing that – the more we can get away from the idea that it is something exceptional, because it patently isn't.

It is interesting that Scotland has done things slightly differently. I can remember going to talk to obstetrics and gynaecological trainees from Scotland. The Scottish trainees were quite vocal and amazed that their English colleagues knew so little. They thought it was awful because for them it was a key part of what they were providing. But it is often the case in gynaecology training now that people do not get the exposure. There's a will to try and make that culture change, to learn from what the independent sector does well and to not see it as separate from other parts of health care.

It is also important to get to midwives to understand different options. There are clearly a group of midwives in the profession now who are very positive about health choices and supporting women whatever their choices. There are also others who do not. Another factor is everybody's willingness to accept the diversity of what people do and don't want to be involved in. Rather than seeing you either don't have any issues around conscience or you are a conscientious objector or whatever terminology you want to use (I understand some people don't like the term 'conscientious objector' in the way that I just have). But I believe there is not enough dialogue around this. We as professionals need to do this more in order not to see things in terms of pathway X or pathway Y, or a person who performs abortions and one who doesn't touch them, or has nothing to do with people who request it.

I work with colleagues who work in abortion care services who are very comfortable doing what they do but there are certain things that they can't or won't do. That's also fine because we all have to accept that everybody's role/position is different. Actually what matters is putting the women first all the time.

Get involved

In Britain

Abortion Rights

Abortion Rights is Britain's national pro-choice campaigning organisation. It was formed in 2003 by the merger between the Abortion Law Reform Association (ALRA) and the National Abortion Campaign (NAC). It organises to defend and extend abortion provision.

www.abortionrights.org.uk
@Abortion_Rights

BPAS

The British Pregnancy Advisory Service provides abortion services and reproductive health care.

www.bpas.org

Doctors for a Woman's Choice on Abortion (DWCA)

DWCA was established in 1976 to campaign for women themselves to have the right to make their own decisions about abortion.

www.dwca.org

Lawyers for Choice

Lawyers for Choice campaigns for the removal of specific criminal prohibitions relating to abortion and for a change in the law to give women the right to make the abortion decision. www.lawyersforchoice.com

Marie Stopes

Marie Stopes UK is the leading independent provider of sexual and reproductive health services in the UK.
www.mariestopes.org.uk

In Northern Ireland

Alliance for Choice

Alliance for Choice leads the fight for free, safe and legal abortions in Northern Ireland.
www.alliance4choice.com

In the Republic of Ireland

Abortion Rights Campaign

The Abortion Rights Campaign is a movement for choice and change in Ireland. It promotes broad national support for a referendum to repeal the 8th Amendment to the Constitution by the Irish Parliament.
www.abortionrightscampaign.ie

Abortion Support Network

Abortion Support Network provides financial assistance and accommodation to women travelling from the Republic of Ireland, Northern Ireland and the Isle of Man to access abortion in Britain.
www.asn.org.uk

Action for Choice

Action for Choice (formally Action on X) is an activist organisation that campaigns for free, safe and legal abortion in Ireland (North and South). It is a member of the Coalition to Repeal the Eighth Amendment.

https://actionforchoice.wordpress.com

Speaking of IMELDA (Ireland Making England the Legal Destination for Abortion)

Speaking of Imelda is direct action feminist performance group. See videos of some of their actions here https://www.youtube.com/channel/UCW_F64htch9WiH5UzONwYQg

https://www.facebook.com/SpeakingofIMELDA/
@speakofIMELDA

The Coalition to Repeal the Eighth

The Coalition to Repeal the Eighth Amendment is a growing alliance of over 70 organisations including human rights, feminist and pro-choice organisations, trade unions, health organisations, NGOs, community organisations and many others committed to changing the law in Ireland.

www.repealeight.ie

X-ile Project

X-ile project is an ongoing online gallery of women who have accessed abortion services outside of Ireland and Northern Ireland.

www.x-ileproject.com

In the US

NARAL Pro-Choice America

The 1.2 million member activists of NARAL Pro-Choice America fight for reproductive freedom for every person in every state.

www.prochoiceamerica.org

Planned Parenthood

Planned Parenthood delivers vital reproductive health care, sex education, and information to millions of women, men, and young people worldwide.

www.plannedparenthood.org

Whole Woman's Health

Whole Woman's Health is a privately owned feminist organisation, committed to providing holistic care for women. It runs a group of women's clinics providing comprehensive gynecology services, including abortion care, in the US.

www.wholewomanshealth.com

Women on Web

Women on Web is a digital community of women who have had abortions, medical doctors, researchers, and individuals and organisations that support abortion rights. It answers thousands of help-emails every day from women around the world. The multi language helpdesk is supervised by medical doctors.

www.womenonweb.org

Women on Waves

Women on Waves aims to prevent unsafe abortions and empower women to exercise their human rights to physical and mental autonomy. It makes sure that women have access to medical abortion and information through innovative strategies.

www.womenonwaves.org

Women Help Women

Women Help Women is an international group of activists, trained counsellors and non-profit organisations and foundations who bridge the gap between reproductive rights, advocacy efforts and service provision.

www.womenhelp.org

Notes

Chapter One

1 www.washingtonpost.com/news/wonk/wp/2016/10/20/rip-the-baby-out-of-the-womb-what-donald-trump-got-wrong-about-abortion-in-america/?utm_term=.762a778ede40.

2 https://mariestopes.org/news/2017/1/re-enactment-of-the-mexico-city-policy/.

3 www.who.int/mediacentre/factsheets/fs388/en/.

4 www.who.int/reproductivehealth/topics/unsafe_abortion/magnitude/en/.

5 www.detroitnews.com/story/news/politics/2016/07/28/pence-trump-will-tap-justices-overturn-abortion-law/87678778/.

6 www.npr.org/2016/10/19/498293478/fact-check-trump-and-clinton-s-final-presidential-debate.

7 https://prh.org/.

8 http://time.com/4651958/mike-pence-anti-abortion-supreme-court-justice-march-for-life/.

9 www.aclu.org/blog/washington-markup/rose-garden-capitol-dark-day-womens-health?emsrc=Nat_Appeal_AutologinEnabled&emissue=trump_administration&emtype=cultivation&ms=eml_170509_cult_gol.

10 https://thefederalist.com/2015/01/22/miscarriage-of-justice-is-big-pharma-breaking-your-uterus/.

11 www.who.int/mediacentre/factsheets/fs388/en/. Published in 2016.

12 www.bpas.org/media/1439/10-abortion-myths-booklet.pdf.

13 www.who.int/medicines/publications/essentialmedicines/18th_EML.pdf.

14 www.scmp.com/article/1003905/late-term-abortion-forced-woman.

15 www.smh.com.au/articles/2002/07/28/1027818485171.html.

16 www.irishtimes.com/news/abortion-worse-than-child-abuse-says-vatican-figure-1.772661.

17 www.pewforum.org/religious-landscape-study/views-about-abortion/.

18 https://yougov.co.uk/news/2010/09/22/arguments-abortion/.

19 www.theguardian.com/world/2016/feb/18/pope-suggests-contraception-can-be-condoned-in-zika-crisis.

20 www.washingtonpost.com/news/morning-mix/wp/2016/02/17/help-zika-in-venezuela-i-need-abortion/?utm_term=.4eb33cf2b00f.

21 www.parliament.uk/documents/lords-committees/Secondary-Legislation-Scrutiny-Committee/SI-376-Ms-Isabelle-Kerr-Submission.pdf.

[22] www.ons.gov.uk/peoplepopulationandcommunity/birthsdeathsandmarriages/families/bulletins/familiesandhouseholds/2016.

[23] www.theguardian.com/world/2017/mar/18/front-national-anger-marine-le-pen-female-supporters.

[24] www.newsweek.com/marine-le-pen-marion-marechal-le-pen-national-front-606487.

[25] This post (and many others) has now been deleted from his website. This link contains the original material: www.mirror.co.uk/news/uk-news/ukip-leader-paul-nuttall-words-9351835.

[26] www.hani.co.kr/arti/english_edition/e_national/766232.html.

[27] http://blog.quipu-project.com/home/.

[28] The author has chosen not to adopt the use of inverted commas around the term race throughout this book. Although race has no scientific basis in biology or genetics the author believes such shorthand can trivialise or invalidate the very real material impact of racism and its consequences.

[29] http://tgeu.org/trans-people-to-receive-compensation-for-forced-sterilisation-in-sweden/.

Chapter Two

[1] http://ipsos-na.com/download/pr.aspx?id=15335.

[2] www.legislation.gov.uk/ukpga/Vict/24-25/100/section/58.

[3] www.liberalhistory.org.uk/wpcontent/uploads/2014/10/14_steel_abortion_reform_1967.pdf.

[4] https://www.gov.uk/government/uploads/system/uploads/attachment_data/file/618533/Abortion_stats_2016_commentary_with_tables.pdf.

[5] https://www.gov.uk/government/uploads/system/uploads/attachment_data/file/618533/Abortion_stats_2016_commentary_with_tables.pdf.

[6] www.belfasttelegraph.co.uk/news/northern-ireland/suicide-risk-to-woman-accused-of-using-poison-to-have-abortion-court-hears-35360082.html.

[7] www.publications.parliament.uk/pa/cm200910/cmselect/cmniaf/236/236we09.htm.

[8] www.health-ni.gov.uk/sites/default/files/publications/dhssps/guidance-termination-pregnancy.pdf.

[9] www.courtsni.gov.uk/en-GB/Judicial%20Decisions/PublishedByYear/Documents/2015/[2015]%20NIQB%2096/j_j_HOR9740Final.htm.

[10] www.courtsni.gov.uk/en-GB/Judicial%20Decisions/PublishedByYear/Documents/2015/[2015]%20NIQB%2096/j_j_HOR9740Final.htm.

[11] www.belfasttelegraph.co.uk/news/northern-ireland/northern-ireland-abortion-reform-mlas-clash-after-amendment-vote-is-defeated-34444332.html.

[12] www.bbc.co.uk/news/uk-northern-ireland-37353825.

[13] https://www.gov.uk/government/uploads/system/uploads/attachment_data/file/618533/Abortion_stats_2016_commentary_with_tables.pdf.

[14] www.supremecourt.uk/cases/docs/uksc-2015-0220-judgment.pdf.

[15] www.ifpa.ie/Hot-Topics/Abortion/Statistics.

16 Irish Family Planning Association (2016) www.ifpa.ie/node/678.
17 https://twitter.com/itstimetorepeal.
18 www.reuters.com/article/us-pope-abortion-idUSKBN13G12B.
19 http://health.gov.ie/wp-content/uploads/2014/09/Guidance-Document-Final-September-2014.pdf.
20 www.bbc.co.uk/news/world-europe-37449903.
21 www.reuters.com/article/us-poland-abortion-idUSTRE67P46Z20100826.
22 www.theguardian.com/world/video/2016/apr/04/polish-women-walk-out-of-church-service-in-protest-against-abortion-ban-video.
23 www.cbsnews.com/news/poland-total-abortion-ban-lesson-humility-mass-protests-women/.
24 www.nytimes.com/2016/01/17/world/europe/on-paper-italy-allows-abortions-but-few-doctors-will-perform-them.html.
25 www.nytimes.com/2016/01/17/world/europe/on-paper-italy-allows-abortions-but-few-doctors-will-perform-them.html.
26 http://wakeupmississippi.org/?page_id=45.
27 www.theguardian.com/world/2016/mar/11/italian-gynaecologists-refuse-abortions-miscarriages.
28 European Committee of Social Rights (2016) https://rm.coe.int/CoERMPublicCommonSearchServices/DisplayDCTMContent?documentId=090000168063ecd7.
29 www.womenonwaves.org/en/page/974/warning--fake-abortion-pills-for-sale-online.
30 www.statnews.com/2016/11/14/medical-abortion-pills-mail/?s_campaign=trendmd.
31 www.tallgirlshorts.net/marymary/gorettitext.html.
32 http://vesselthefilm.com/.
33 www.womenonwaves.org/en/page/934/in-collection/483/european-court-rules-that-portugal-violated-freedom-of-expression-of-women-on-wa.
34 www.bbc.co.uk/news/uk-northern-ireland-39259616.

Chapter Three

1 www.iwm.org.uk.
2 www.iwm.org.uk/history/what-was-the-womens-land-army; www.nationalarchives.gov.uk/womeninuniform/wwii_intro.htm.

Chapter Four

1 www.bmj.com/content/349/bmj.g4770.
2 news.bbc.co.uk/onthisday/hi/dates/stories/december/29/newsid_2547000/2547249.stm.
3 www.abortionrights.org.uk/dilys-cossey-ar-agm-speech-agm-honouring-the-legacy-of-alra/.
4 www.lesleyahall.net/abortion.htm.

5 www.screenonline.org.uk/tv/id/440997/.
6 www.theguardian.com/media/2002/apr/16/pressandpublishing2.
7 www.abortionrights.org.uk/dilys-cossey-ar-agm-speech-agm-honouring-the-legacy-of-alra/.
8 http://hansard.millbanksystems.com/commons/1967/jul/13/clause-4-conscientious-objection-to.
9 http://hansard.millbanksystems.com/commons/1967/jul/13/clause-4-conscientious-objection-to.
10 For more on SPUC, see Chapter Five.
11 http://hansard.millbanksystems.com/commons/1967/jul/13/clause-4-conscientious-objection-to.
12 www.legislation.gov.uk/ukpga/1929/34/pdfs/ukpga_19290034_en.pdf.

Chapter Five

1 www.heraldscotland.com/news/15070358.US anti-abortion protests targeting four major Scots hospitals/?c=s9lrno#cbmments-anchor.
2 www.spuc.org.uk/abortion/pro-life-feminism.
3 www.independent.co.uk/news/science/the-lost-girls-illegal-abortion-widely-used-by-some-uk-ethnic-groups-to-avoid-daughters-has-reduced-9059790.html.
4 https://www.gov.uk/government/uploads/system/uploads/attachment_data/file/200527/Gender_birth_ratio_in_the_UK.pdf.
5 www.abortionrights.org.uk/press-release-glenda-jackson-diane-abbott-oppose-trojan-horse-amendment/.
6 https://rewire.news/article/2014/03/12/sex-selective-abortion-bans-highlight-faultlines-reproductive-rights-movement/.
7 http://test.abortionrights.org.uk/wp-content/uploads/2014/09/AR%20Position%20Statement-Disability%20pdf.pdf.
8 https://www.gov.uk/government/uploads/system/uploads/attachment_data/file/618533/Abortion_stats_2016_commentary_with_tables.pdf.
9 www.bbc.co.uk/news/uk-politics-14817816.
10 https://thinkprogress.org/study-even-when-abortion-inspires-mixed-emotions-women-say-it-was-the-right-decision-for-them-cfca0bad94b9.
11 www.bbc.co.uk/news/uk-39472417.
12 www.huffingtonpost.co.uk/kerry-abel/using-the-tampon-tax-to-f_b_15813746.html.
13 www.reuters.com/article/us-ultrasound-abortion-idUSBREA0T1PC20140130.
14 www.scribd.com/document/96958198/Facts-Speak-Louder-Than-the-Silent-Scream-03-02.
15 www.rcog.org.uk/globalassets/documents/guidelines/rcogfetalawarenesswpr0610.pdf.
16 www.independent.co.uk/news/world/americas/us-republican-justin humphrey-oklahoma-abortion-Iaw-sex-planne -parenthood-pro-choice a7580326.html.

17 www.cdc.gov/mmwr/preview/mmwrhtml/ss6410a1.htm?s_cid=ss6410a1_e.

18 https://www.gov.uk/government/uploads/system/uploads/attachment_data/file/618533/Abortion_stats_2016_commentary_with_tables.pdf.

19 www.bbc.co.uk/news/health-19854465.

20 www.theguardian.com/commentisfree/2014/aug/31/abortion-media-reflect-real-world-right-to-choose.

21 http://abort67.co.uk/blog/expectant-mums-we-need-your-help#sthash.GRlZiKJr.dpuf ho.

22 www.nytimes.com/2016/06/28/us/supreme-court-texas-abortion.html.

23 www.nytimes.com/2016/06/28/us/supreme-court-texas-abortion.html.

24 www.reproductiverights.org/sites/crr.civicactions.net/files/documents/USPA_StateofStates_11.16_Web_Final.pdf.

25 www.motherjones.com/mixed-media/2011/04/mother-sues-anti-abortion-groups-billboards.

26 http://abc7ny.com/archive/7974303/.

27 www.politicalresearch.org/2010/04/29/abortion-as-black-genocide-an-old-scare-tactic-re-emerges/#sthash.YXS1ElUS.dpbs.

28 www.nydailynews.com/news/nationalfanti-:abortion-billboards georgia-claim-black-children-endangered-species-article-1.168088.

29 https://napawf.org/wp-content/uploads/2011/12/PreNDA-Letter-RJ-Orgs.pdf.

30 www.guttmacher.org/news-release/2017/abortion-coverage-restrictions-affect-millions-women.

31 Reported in *Socialist Worker* (1979).

32 www.tuc.org.uk/equality-issues/gender-equality/abortion-rights.

33 www.abortionrights.org.uk/wp-content/uploads/2015/08/AR-Student-campus-document-alt-footer.pdf.

34 www.abortionrights.org.uk/wp-content/uploads/2015/08/AR-Student-campus-document-alt-footer.pdf.

35 www.birminghammail.co.uk/news/midlands-news/watch-angry-scenes-anti-abortionists-11332807.

36 http://news.bbc.co.uk/1/hi/uk_politics/7449268.stm.

Chapter Six

1 www.fawcettsociety.org.uk/policy-research/the-gender-pay-gap/.

2 www.bbc.co.uk/news/uk-39416554.

3 www.bbc.co.uk/news/uk-politics-36760986.

4 http://nytlive.nytimes.com/womenintheworld/2017/01/23/british-prime-minister-theresa-may-will-not-confront-trump-about-sexism/.

5 www.theguardian.com/us-news/video/2017/jan/27/trump-may-hold-hands-white-house-video.

6 http://hansard.millbanksystems.com/commons/1981/nov/04/latchkey-children.

7 www.publications.parliament.uk/pa/cm201516/cmhansrd/cm151125/debtext/151125-0001.htm.
8 www.tuc.org.uk/sites/default/files/MotherhoodPayPenalty.pdf.
9 www.theguardian.com/money/2014/aug/12/managers-avoid-hiring-younger-women-maternity-leave.
10 www.publications.parliament.uk/pa/cm201617/cmselect/cmwomeq/90/9002.htm?utm_source=90&utm_medium=fullbullet&utm_campaign=modulereports.
11 www.ageuk.org.uk/Documents/EN-GB/Campaigns/Care%20in%20Crisis%20-%20FINAL.pdf?dtrk=true.
12 www.theguardian.com/technology/2014/oct/15/apple-facebook-offer-freeze-eggs-female-employees.
13 www.eggbanxx.com/events.
14 movementforanadoptionapology.org.
15 www.theguardian.com/society/2016/nov/04/baby-adoption-practices-of-past-demand-inquiry-say-law-firms.
16 www.theguardian.com/society/2016/nov/04/baby-adoption-practices-of-past-demand-inquiry-say-law-firms.
17 www.thejournal.ie/us-adoptions-ireland-1950s-royal-irish-academy-3150953-Jan2017/?utm_source=shortlink.
18 www.thejournal.ie/us-adoptions-ireland-1950s-royal-irish-academy-3150953-Jan2017/?utm_source=shortlink.
19 www.bbc.co.uk/news/world-europe-39254784.
20 www.lennonwylie.co.uk/bobpage429.htm.
21 www.lennonwylie.co.uk/bobpage429.htm.
22 www.magdalenelaundries.com/index.htm.
23 www.bbc.co.uk/news/world-europe-17509593.
24 http://symphysiotomyireland.com/the-story/).
25 www.independent.co.uk/news/fury-over-lunch-hour-abortions-1258286.html.
26 www.theguardian.com/society/2010/jun/06/rachel-cooke-fifty-years-the-pill-oral-contraceptive.

Chapter Seven

1 www.rcm.org.uk/news-views-and-analysis/news/rcm-position-statement-on-abortion.
2 https://kar.kent.ac.uk/51585/1/__bodiam_HHR_sg575_My%20Files_S%20Sheldon%20Regulatory%20Cliff-edge%20JME.pdf.
3 http://mashable.com/2016/03/01/abortion-stigma-whole-womans-health/.
4 www.twitter.com/TwoWomenTravel; www.shoutyourabortion.com.
5 www.scotsman.com/news/education/snp-urged-to-make-sex-education-compulsory-1-4334337; www.walesonline.co.uk/news/wales-news/wales-should-follow-englands-lead-12712239.
6 www.barnardos.org.uk/news/Children_want_safer_lives/latest-news.htm?ref=121054).

7 www.cpag.org.uk/child-poverty-facts-and-figures.
8 www.wateraid.org/what-we-do/the-crisis/statistics.

Bibliography

Aiken, ARA, Gomperts, R and Trussell, J (2016) 'Experiences and characteristics of women seeking and completing at-home medical termination of pregnancy through online telemedicine in Ireland and Northern Ireland: a population-based analysis', *BJOG*, doi: 10.1111/1471-0528.14401.

Aiken, ARA, Digol, I, Trussell, J, Gomperts, J (2017) 'Self reported outcomes and adverse events after medical abortion through online telemedicine: population based study in the Republic of Ireland and Northern Ireland', *BMJ*, 357: j2011, www.bmj.com/content/357/bmj.j2011.

Alaimo, S, (2000) *Undomesticated ground: Recasting nature as feminist space*, Ithaca, NY: Cornell University Press.

Aldgate, A (1995) *Censorship and permissive society*, Oxford: Clarendon Press.

Amnesty International (2016a) 'Irish public want expanded access to abortion to be a political priority for incoming government' (4 March), www.amnesty.org/en/latest/news/2016/03/irish-public-want-expanded-access-to-be-a-political-priority-for-incoming-government/.

Amnesty International (2016b) 'Northern Ireland: nearly 3/4 of public support abortion law change – new poll' (18 October), www.amnesty.org.uk/press-releases/northern-ireland-nearly-34-public-support-abortion-law-change-new-poll-0.

Astbury-Ward, E (2015) 'Abortion "on the NHS": the National Health Service and abortion stigma', *Journal of Family Planning and Reproductive Health Care*, 41:3, 168–9.

Balfour, L (1979) 'Time to shout', *Socialist Worker*, 27 October, p 9.

Banyard, K (2010) *The equality illusion: The truth about women and men today*, London: Faber and Faber.

Barker, TC and Drake, M (eds) (1982) *Population and society in Britain, 1850–1980*, London: Batsford Academic and Educational.

Baron, C, Cameron, S and Johnstone, A (2015) 'Do women seeking termination of pregnancy need pre-abortion counselling?' *Journal Family Planning Reproductive Health Care*, 41:3, 181–5.

Berg, M (2016) www.plannedparenthoodaction.org/blog/8-outrageous-facts-about-mike-pencerecord-reproductive-rights.

Biggs, MA, Upadhyay, UD, McCulloch, CE and Foster, DG (2016) 'Women's mental health and well-being 5 years after receiving or being denied an abortion: a prospective, longitudinal cohort study', *JAMA Psychiatry*, 14 December, doi: 10.1001/jamapsychiatry.2016.3478.

Bland, L (2002) *Banishing the beast: Feminism, sex and morality*, London: Tauris Parke Paperbacks.

BPAS (2015) *Abortion: Trusting women to decide and doctors to practise*, Stratford-upon-Avon: BPAS.

Brooke, S (2002) 'ICBH witness seminar: The Abortion Act 1967' (2001), Institute of Contemporary British History, www.kcl.ac.uk/sspp/departments/icbh/witness/PDFfiles/AbortionAct1967.pdf.

Brooke, S (2013) *Sexual politics: Sexuality, family planning, and the British left from the 1880s to the present day*, Oxford: Oxford University Press.

Brookes, B (2013) *Abortion in England 1900–1967*, London: Croom Helm.

Brooks, L (2014) 'Catholic midwives' abortion ruling overturned by Supreme Court', *The Guardian* (17 December), www.theguardian.com/world/2014/dec/17/catholic-midwives-abortion-ruling-overturned.

Bryant, A, Narasimhan, S, Bryant-Comstock, K and Levi, EE (2014) 'Crisis pregnancy center websites: information, misinformation and disinformation', *Contraception*, 90:6, 601–5.

Cashdan, E (1985) 'Natural fertility, birth spacing, and the "first demographic transition"', *American Anthropologist*, 87:3, 650–3.

Cliff, T (1978) *Revolution besieged*, London: Pluto Press.

Cook, RJ, Erdman, JN and Dickens, BM (eds) (2014) *Abortion law in transnational perspective: Cases and controversies*, Philadelphia, PA: University of Pennsylvania Press.

Coote, A and Campbell, B (1987) *Sweet freedom*, Oxford: Blackwell.

Cossey, D (2002) 'ICBH witness seminar: The Abortion Act 1967' (2001), Institute of Contemporary British History, www.kcl.ac.uk/sspp/departments/icbh/witness/PDFfiles/AbortionAct1967.pdf.

Criado-Perez, C (2015) *Do it like a woman ... And change the world*, London: Portobello Books.

Dangerfield, G (1997) *The strange death of liberal England*, London: Serif.

Davis, A (1981) *Women, race, and class*, New York: Random House.

Devereux, G (1960) *A study of abortion in primitive societies: A typological, distributional, and dynamic analysis of the prevention of birth in 400 preindustrial societies*, London: Thomas Yoseloff Ltd.

Digby, A and Stewart, J (1998) *Gender, health and welfare*, London: Taylor & Francis.

Donovan, M (2017) 'In real life: federal restrictions on abortion coverage and the women they impact', *Guttmacher Policy Review*, 20. www.guttmacher.org/gpr/2017/01/real-life-federal-restrictions-abortion-coverage-and-women-they-impact.

Dowsing, S (2000) *Contraception and abortion in the early Roman Empire: A critical examination of ancient sources and modern interpretations*, MA Thesis, Ottawa: University of Ottawa.

Drake, B (1984) *Women in the trade unions*, London: Virago.

Draper, E (1972) *Birth control in the modern world: The role of the individual in population control* (2nd edn), London: Penguin.

Dyhouse, C (2013) *Girl trouble: Panic and progress in the history of young women*, London: Palgrave Macmillan.

Education for Choice (2012) *Abortion education in the UK: Failing our young people?* www.brook.org.uk/images/brook/professionals/documents/page_content/EFC/abortioneducationreport.pdf.

Education for Choice (2014) *Crisis pregnancy centres: Highlighting misinformation, bias and poor quality practice in independent pregnancy counselling centres in the UK*, London: Brook.

Ehrenreich, B and English, D (1973) *Witches, midwives, and nurses: A history of women healers*, New York: The Feminist Press.
Eisenstein, H (2009) *Feminism seduced*, London: Paradigm.
Elderton, E (1914) *Report on the English birthrate,* London: Cambridge University Press.
Empson, M (2014) *Land and labour*, London: Bookmarks Publications.
Engels, F (1973) *The condition of the working class in Britain*, London: Lawrence and Wishart.
Faludi, S (1992) *Backlash: The undeclared war against women*, London: Chatto & Windus.
Ferris, P (1966) *The nameless:Abortion in Britain today*, London: Hutchinson and co.
Fitzgerald, C (2016) 'Ireland has been told by the UN Human Rights Council to change its abortion laws' (13 May), www.thejournal.ie/ireland-hum-rights-2768942-May2016/.
Flannery, K and Marcus, J (2012) *The creation of inequality*, London: Harvard University Press.
Foot, P (2012) *The vote: How it was won and how it was undermined*, London: Bookmarks.
Francombe, C (1984) *Abortion freedom: A worldwide movement*, London: HarperCollins.
Fried, MG (ed) (1990) *From abortion to reproductive freedom: Transforming a movement*, Boston, MA: South End Press.
Fryer, P (1965) *The birth controllers*, London: Secker & Warburg.
Furedi, A (2016) *The moral case for abortion*, London: Palgrave Macmillan.
Furedi, A and Hume, M (1997) *Abortion law reformers: Pioneers of change*, London: Birth Control Trust.
Gaffin, J. and Thoms, D (1983) *Caring & sharing: The centenary history of the Co-operative Women's Guild*, Manchester: Co-operative Union.
Gentleman, A (2016) 'Northern Irish women ask to be prosecuted for taking abortion pills', *The Guardian* (23 May), www.theguardian.com/world/2016/may/23/northern-ireland-women-ask-to-be-prosecuted-for-taking-abortion-pills.
Gittins, D (1982) *Fair sex: Family size and structure, 1900–39*, London: Hutchinson.

Gordon, L (1990) *Woman's body, woman's right*, New York: Penguin.

Grahame, H (1989) *Out of the back streets: PAS, 21 years of service to women*, London: Pregnancy Advisory Service.

Greenwood, V and Young, J (1976) *Abortion on demand*, London: Pluto Press.

Grimes, MDA and Brandon, LG (2014) *Every third woman in America: How legal abortion transformed our nation*, Carolina Beach: Daymark Publishing.

Hall, A and Ransom, WB (1906) 'Plumbism from the ingestion of diachylon as an abortifacient', *British Medical Journal*, 1:2, 356, 428–30.

Hall, LA (2011) *The life and times of Stella Browne: Feminist and free spirit*, London: IB Tauris.

Hall, LA (ed) (2005) *Outspoken women: An anthology of women's writing on sex, 1870–1969*, London: Routledge.

Hall, VG (2013) *Women at work, 1860–1939: How different industries shaped women's experiences*, Rochester, NY: The Boydell Press.

Halpin, M and O'Grady, P (2016) 'Equality, democracy, solidarity: the politics of abortion', *Irish Marxist Review*, 5: 16, www.irishmarxistreview.net/index.php/imr/article/viewFile/212/204.

Harker, R (2016) *Statistics on abortion: Briefing paper 04418* (12 December), London: House of Commons Library.

Harman, C, (1999) *The people's history of the world*, London: Bookmarks Publications.

Hayes, G and Lowe, P (2015) *A hard enough decision to make: Anti-abortion activism outside clinics in the eyes of clinic users*, Birmingham: Aston University.

Hindell, K and Simms, M (1971) *Abortion law reformed*, London: Peter Owen.

Hoggart, L (2010) *Feminist principles meet political reality: The case of the National Abortion Campaign*, www.prochoiceforum.org.uk/al6.php.

Holdsworth, A (1988) *Out of the doll's house: The story of women in the twentieth century*, London: BBC Books.

Horgan, G and O'Connor, JS (2014) 'Abortion and citizenship rights in a devolved region of the UK', *Social Policy and Society*, 13: 1, 39–49.

Humphries, S (1989) *Secret world of sex: Sex before marriage – the British experience, 1900–1950*, London: Sidgwick & Jackson.

Humphries, S and Gordon, P (1994) *Forbidden Britain*, London: BBC Books.

If/When/How (2016) *Women of color and the struggle for reproductive justice*, Oakland: Lawyering for Reproductive Justice.

Ipas (2010) *The evidence speaks for itself: Ten facts about abortion*, Chapel Hill, NC: Ipas.

Jenkins, A (1960) *Law for the rich*, London: Victor Gollancz.

Jones, L and Pemberton, N (2014) 'Ten Rillington Place and the changing politics of abortion in modern Britain', *Historical Journal*, 57: 4, 1085–109.

Jytte, R and Russell, V (2008) *Contraception: A history*, Cambridge: Polity Press.

Kacpura, K (2016a) 'This victory on abortion has empowered Polish women – we'll never be the same', *The Guardian* (6 October), www.theguardian.com/commentisfree/2016/oct/06/victory-abortion-rights-empowered-polish-women.

Kacpura, K (2016b) 'Stop this crackdown on abortion in Poland', *The Guardian* (21 September), www.theguardian.com/commentisfree/2016/sep/21/stop-abortion-law-crackdown-poland-reproductive-rights.

Kacpura, K, Więckiewicz, K, Jawień, B, Grzywacz, A and Zimniewska, M (2013) *Twenty years of anti-abortion law in Poland*, Warsaw: Federation for Women and Family Planning.

Kaplan, L (1997) *The story of Jane: The legendary underground feminist abortion service*, Chicago: Chicago University Press.

Katz Rothman, B (1992) 'Plenary address: Midwives Alliance of North America, New York', in Davis-Floyd, RE and Sargent, C (1997) *Childbirth and authoritative knowledge: Cross-cultural perspectives*, Oakland, CA: University of California Press.

Kirchgaessner, S, Duncan, P, Nardelli, A and Robineau, D (2016) 'Seven in 10 Italian gynaecologists refuse to carry out abortions', *The Guardian* (11 March), www.theguardian.com/world/2016/mar/11/italian-gynaecologists-refuse-abortions-miscarriages.

Klein, Y Ed (1997) *Beyond the home front: Women's autobiographical writing of the Two World Wars*, New York: New York University Press.

Knight, P (1977) 'Women and abortion in Victorian and Edwardian England', *History Workshop Journal*, 4, 57-68.

Koblitz, AH (2014) *Sex and herbs and birth control: Women and fertility regulation through the ages*, Seattle: Kovalevskaia Fund.

Layland, W and Economou, GD (1996) *William Langland's Piers Plowman: The C Version* (The Middle Ages Series), Philadelphia: University of Pennsylvania Press.

Lewis, J (1984) *Women in England, 1870–1950: Sexual divisions and social change*, Brighton: Harvester Press.

Liddington, J and Norris, J (2000) *One hand tied behind us: The rise of the women's suffrage movement*, London: Rivers Oram Press.

Limbrick, G (2014) *Unlocked: Hidden stories of the lives of Birmingham women 1900 to the present day*, Birmingham: Library of Birmingham.

Livengood, C and Christine Ferretti, C (2016) 'Pence: abortion law will end in history's "ash heap"', *Detroit News* (29 July), www.detroitnews.com/story/news/politics/2016/07/28/pence-trump-will-tap-justices-overturn-abortion-law/87678778/.

Longmate, N (2002) *How we lived then: A history of everyday life during the Second World War*, London: Pimlico.

Luker, K (1992) *Abortion and the politics of motherhood*, Berkeley, CA: University of California Press.

Marie Stopes International (2007) www.shnwales.org.uk/Documents/485/Report,%20GPs%20attitudes%20to%20abortion%202007%20Marie%20Stopes.pdf.

Marlow, J (1998) *The Virago book of women and the Great War*, London: Virago Press.

McDermid, J and Anna Hillyar, A (1999) *Midwives of the revolution: Female Bolsheviks and women workers 1917*, London: UCL Press.

McLaren, A (1978) *Birth control in nineteenth-century England: A social and intellectual history*, London: Croom Helm.

McLaren, A (1984) *Reproductive rituals: Perceptions of fertility in Britain from the 16th century to the 19th century*, London: Methuen Young Books.

Moran, C (2011) *How to be a woman*, London: Ebury Press.

Munday, D (2017) Interview with author, at interviewee's home, January.

NAC (National Abortion Campaign) (1992) *A celebration of 25 years of safe legal abortion 1967–1992*, London: National Abortion Campaign.

Nelson, J (2003) *Women of color and the reproductive rights movement*, New York: New York University Press.

O'Regan, E (2013) 'More than 100 psychiatrists disagree with abortion proposal', *Irish News* (25 April), www.independent.ie/irish-news/more-than-100-psychiatrists-disagree-with-abortion-proposal-29222046.html.

Okamoto, E (2014) 'Japan turns pro-life: recent change in reproductive health policy and challenges by new technologies', *International Journal of Health Policy and Management*, 2: 2, 61–3.

Ormston, R and Curtice, J (eds) (2015) *British social attitudes: The 32nd report*, London: NatCen Social Research.

Paintin, D (1998) 'A medical view of abortion in the 1960s', in Lee, E (ed.) *Abortion law and politics today*, London: Macmillan Press, pp 12-19.

Pandit, E (2014) 'Sex-selective abortion bans highlight faultlines in the reproductive rights movement', *Rewire*, 12 March, https://rewire.news/article/2014/03/12/sex-selective-abortion-bans-highlight-faultlines-reproductive-rights-movement/.

Pearson, H (2015) www.abortionrights.org.uk/scottish-women-face-significant-barriers-access-to-abortion-in-scotland/.

Petchesky, RP (1986) *Abortion and woman's choice: The state, sexuality and reproductive freedom*, London: Verso.

Petchesky, RP (1987) 'Fetal images: the power of visual culture in the politics of reproduction', *Feminist Studies*, 13: 2, 263–92.

Pianigiani, G (2016) 'On paper, Italy allows abortions, but few doctors will perform them', *The New York Times* (16 January), www.nytimes.com/2016/01/17/world/europe/on-paper-italy-allows-abortions-but-few-doctors-will-perform-them.html?_r=0.

Pinchbeck, I (1977) *Women workers and the Industrial Revolution 1750–1850*, London: Frank Cass and co.

Pollitt, K (2015) *Pro: reclaiming abortion rights*, New York: Picador USA.

Porter, C (2013) *Alexandra Kollontai*, Pontypool: The Merlin Press.

Potts, M, Diggory, P, Peel, J (1977) *Abortion*, New York: Cambridge University Press.

Purcell, C, Hilton, S, and McDaid, L (2014) 'The stigmatisation of abortion: a qualitative analysis of print media in Great Britain in 2010', *Culture, Health and Sexuality*, 16: 9, 1141–55.

Raw, L (2011) *Striking a light: The Bryant and May Matchwomen and their place in history*, London: Continuum.

Richardson, J (1988), 'The battles in parliament', *NAC News* 5, Spring, p 12.

Riddle, JM (1992) *Contraception and abortion from the Ancient World to the Renaissance* (3rd edn), Cambridge, MA: Harvard University Press.

Riddle, JM (1997) *Eve's herbs: A history of contraception and abortion in the West*, Cambridge: Harvard University Press.

Roberts, E (1984) *A woman's place: An oral history of working class women 1890–1940*, Oxford: Blackwell.

Roberts, E (1999) *Women and families: An oral history, 1940–1970*, Oxford: Blackwell.

Rose, L (1986) *Massacre of the innocents: Infanticide in Britain, 1800–1939*, London: Routledge & Kegan Paul Books.

Rosen, H (ed) (1967) *Abortion in America*, Boston: Beacon.

Rosenberg, C (1989) *Women and perestroika*, London: Bookmarks Publications.

Rowbotham, S (1977) *A new world for women: Stella Browne, socialist feminist*, London: Pluto Press.

Rowbotham, S (1977a) *Hidden from history: 300 years of women's oppression and the fight against it* (3rd edn), London: Pluto Press.

Rowbotham, S (1999) *A century of women*, London: Penguin Books.

Rowbotham, S (2010) *Dreamers of a new day: Women who invented the twentieth century*, London: Verso.

Rowe, M (ed) (1984) *Spare Rib Reader*, London: Penguin.

Royal College of Obstetricians and Gynaecologists (RCOG) (2007) www.rcog.org.uk/en/news/rcog-statement-on-article-abortion-crisis-as-doctors-refuse-to-perform-surgery-independent-16-april-2007/.

Ryan, M, Edgecombe, M and Chance, J (1947) *Back street surgery*, Fordingbridge: ALRA.

Schneir, M (ed) (1995) *The Vintage book of feminism*, London: Vintage.

Schoen, J (2005) *Choice and coercion: Birth control, sterilization, and abortion in public health and welfare*, New York: University of North Carolina Press.

Seal, V (1990) *Whose choice? Working-class women and the control of fertility*, Minneapolis: Fortress Books.

Sheldon, S (1997) *Beyond control: Medical power and abortion law*, London: Pluto Press.

Sheldon, S (2015) 'The regulatory cliff edge between contraception and abortion: the legal and moral significance of implantation', *Journal of Medical Ethics*, https://kar.kent.ac.uk/51585/1/__bodiam_HHR_sg575_My%20Files_S%20Sheldon%20Regulatory%20Cliff-edge%20JME.pdf

Sheldon, S (2016) 'How can a state control swallowing? The home use of abortion pills in Ireland', *Reproductive Health Matters*, 24:48, 90-101.

Sheldon, S (2017) 'Abortion law reform in Victoria: lessons for the UK', *Journal of Family Planning and Reproductive Health Care*, 43, 25.

Sherwood, H (2016) 'Baby adoption practices of past demand inquiry, say law firms', *The Guardian* (4 November), www.theguardian.com/society/2016/nov/04/baby-adoption-practices-of-past-demand-inquiry-say-law-firms.

Shorter, E (1984) *A history of women's bodies*, London: Penguin.

Shrage, L (2002) 'From reproductive rights to reproductive Barbie: post-porn modernism and abortion', *Feminist Studies*, 28: 1, 61 –93.

Smith, I (2015) 'How one women's group took on anti-abortion protesters at their local clinic', *Broadly* (21 December), https://broadly.vice.com/en_us/article/how-one-womens-group-took-on-anti-abortion-protesters-at-their-local-clinic.

Socialist Worker (1979) 3 November.

Steel, D (2002) 'ICBH witness seminar: The Abortion Act 1967' (2001), Institute of Contemporary British History, www.kcl.ac.uk/sspp/departments/icbh/witness/PDFfiles/AbortionAct1967.pdf.

Strickland, SLM (2011) 'Conscientious objection in medical students: a questionnaire survey', *Journal of Medical Ethics*, 38: 1, http://jme.bmj.com/content/38/1/22.full.pdf+html.

Thomson, M (2013) 'Abortion law and professional boundaries', *Social & Legal Studies*, 22: 2, 191–210.

Thurtle, D (1940) *Abortion: right or wrong?*, London: T Werner Laurie.

Tilley, E, Earle, S, Walmsley, J and Atkinson, D (2012) 'The silence is roaring: sterilization, reproductive rights and women with intellectual disabilities', *Disability and Society*, 27: 3, 413–26.

Tyler, I (2008) 'Chav mum chav scum', *Feminist Media Studies*, 8:1, 17–34.

Vandewalker, I. (2012) 'Abortion and informed consent: how biased counseling laws mandate violations of medical ethics', *Michigan Journal of Gender and Law*, 19:1, 2–70.

Weeks, J (1981) *Sex, politics and society*, London: Longman.

White, K (2000) *Sexual liberation or sexual license? The American revolt against Victorianism*, Chicago, IL: Ivan R. Dee.

Widgery, D (1975) 'Abortion: the pioneers', *International Socialism* (1st series) 80: July/August, 6–11, www.marxists.org/archive/widgery/1975/07/abortion.htm.

Witness Seminar: The Abortion Act 1967 (2001), Institute of Contemporary British History, www.kcl.ac.uk/sspp/departments/icbh/witness/PDFfiles/AbortionAct1967.pdf.

Wolf, A (2013) *The XX factor: How working women are creating a new society*, London: Profile Books.

Women's Cooperative Guild (1915) *Maternity: Letters from working women*, London: Bell and Sons.

Woodside, M (1966) *Abortion in Britain: Proceedings of a conference held by the Family Planning Association at the University of London Union*, London: Pitman Medical Publishing.

Zebrowski, A. (2016) 'Fight for abortion rights explodes onto Poland's streets', *Socialist Worker*, 3 October, https://socialistworker.co.uk/art/43458/Fight+for+abortion+rights+explodes+onto+Polands+streets.

Index

H

I

J

K

L

O

P

R

Z